Foreword

Our story is about the first letter written by the Christian apostle Paul to his converts at Corinth, a letter full of practical counsel and instruction that reflects deep conflicts within the church there. It is the only letter from Paul that provides significant evidence of the early history of the Christian church. In the past, theologians, beginning with Clement, have read and used it, especially when they too were concerned with administrative and disciplinary problems. Gnostic or semi-Gnostic exegetes found it difficult to understand, as we see from the Valentinian Gnostics, especially as discussed by Irenaeus, and the controversial heretic Tatian.[1] In the ancient church, its best interpreter was John Chrysostom, the practical pastor, preacher, and ascetic who became patriarch of Constantinople in the fourth century.[2]

But there is more to the story of Corinthian Christians than 1 Corinthians, even if we include the more personal 2 Corinthians with it. There is the archaeology of Corinth, carried on especially by American excavators during the last century. There is the Greco-Roman context of Corinth as a newly Romanized Greek city in the early Roman Empire. And there is the Christian context of 1 Corinthians, found in the administrative and liturgical aspects of early church history. Much has been studied; much remains to be done. This study tries to understand the several contexts of the Corinthian Christians.

My concern for 1 Corinthians dates from 1938, when I

studied it under W. H. P. Hatch at the Episcopal Theological School in Cambridge, Massachusetts. A couple of years later, I examined papyri under the guidance of W. L. Westermann at Columbia University, and then worked at the Harvard Divinity School from 1941 to 1944 under the direction of H. J. Cadbury, A. D. Nock, and W. Jaeger. First Corinthians was the first Pauline letter I taught in 1944 at the School of Theology of the University of the South. I have found out more about it since then, thanks recently to references generously supplied by Elizabeth R. Gebhard of the University of Chicago Isthmia excavations.

PAUL IN THE ROMAN WORLD

The Conflict at Corinth

Robert M. Grant

Westminster John Knox Press
LOUISVILLE
LONDON • LEIDEN

© 2001 Robert M. Grant

Scripture quotations from the New Revised Standard Version of the Bible are copyright © 1989 by the Division of Christian Education of the National Council of the Churches of Christ in the U.S.A. and are used by permission.

Book design by Sharon Adams
Cover design by Terry Dugan Design

First edition
Published by Westminster John Knox Press
Louisville, Kentucky

This book is printed on acid-free paper that meets the American National Standards Institute Z39.48 standard.♾

PRINTED IN THE UNITED STATES OF AMERICA

01 02 03 04 05 06 07 08 09 10 — 10 9 8 7 6 5 4 3 2 1

Library of Congress Cataloging-in-Publication Data

Grant, Robert McQueen, 1917–

    Paul in the Roman world : the conflict at Corinth / by Robert M. Grant.—1st ed.
       p. cm.
    Includes bibliographical references and index.
    ISBN 0-664-22452-0 (pbk. : alk. paper)
    1. Bible. N.T. Corinthians—Criticism, interpretation, etc. 2. Corinth (Greece)—Religious life and customs. 3. Corinth (Greece)—Social life and customs. 4. Corinth (Greece)—Social conditions. 5. Corinth (Greece)—Church history. 6. Church his-tory—Primitive and early church, ca. 30–600. I. Title.

BS2675.2 .G73 2001
227'.2067—dc21

2001023392

PAUL IN THE ROMAN WORLD

Part I

Business and Politics

Contents

1

The Journey to Corinth

Paul's Gospel at Thessalonica

When the Christian apostle Paul traveled from northern to southern Greece in the winter of 49/50, he addressed prospective converts in the cities of Philippi (Acts 16:12–40), Thessalonica (17:1–9), Athens, and Corinth. From Corinth he sent back a pastoral letter to the Thessalonians,[1] recalling how they "turned to God from idols, to serve a living and true God, and to wait for his Son from heaven, whom he raised from the dead—Jesus, who rescues us from the wrath that is coming" (1 Thess. 1:9–10). He then emphasized four main points: (1) his gospel as contrasted with idolatry, (2) the kind of marital behavior required of converts, (3) the necessity of work, and (4) the impending return of Jesus from heaven. These points do not reflect the semiphilosophical concerns found in the letters to the Corinthians, but they offer significant insights into Paul's ideas when he was writing.

Everything in Paul's sentence about the conversion of the Thessalonians would have been clear to a Jew or a Jewish Christian, but would have needed to be explained to a Gentile. To a Jewish hearer, Paul's proclamation would make sense because the Old Testament prophets had proclaimed the moral demands of God, had insisted that his wrath was due against disobedience, and had spoken of a mysterious "servant" (probably Israel) who would suffer on behalf of the people and win God's forgiveness. Jews had heard of God's creative and caring actions for the people. God was obviously real and living, and announced himself as the only God. He chose individuals, addressing them as sons; he promised resurrection; and he took the prophet Elijah up into heaven at death (1 Kings 2:11). Paul was proud of his Jewish ancestry, as he told the Galatians: "I advanced in Judaism beyond many among my people of the same age, for I was far more zealous for the traditions of my ancestors" (Gal. 1:14). He was going to preach to the Gentiles simply because the God who had set him apart as a Jew from birth had now called him to this task.

In 1 Thessalonians 2:14–16, however, he harshly criticizes "the Jews," who "killed both the Lord Jesus and the prophets, and drove us out; they displease God and oppose everyone by hindering us from speaking to the Gentiles so that they may be saved. Thus, they have constantly been filling up the measure of their sins; but God's wrath has overtaken them at last." He was adversely affected by Jewish opposition to his mission at Thessalonica, which he interpreted as opposition to God and humanity. His self-esteem momentarily betrayed him into generalizing too much (see chapter 3).

In any event, the more intelligent Gentiles would have found his attack on paganism pointless. They did not worship idols but found in them the symbols of a higher and more spiritual faith. They could hardly accept the notion that the God of Jews and Christians was living and real while the other gods were not, and the notion that a dead man was alive in heaven and would come back was unacceptable. It would be absurd to suppose that someone named Jesus was such a person. Finally, how this Jesus would deliver one from wrath was highly dubious, even supposing that there was such a thing as divine wrath. Most philosophers agreed that the primitive stories of mythology told about divine wrath only superficially. These stories must have had some deeper, more philosophical meaning. In any case, why would God or the gods be angry with human beings? What justification was there for wrath, especially since in mythology the gods behaved so much like human beings?

Further on in his letter, Paul emphasizes another aspect of the Christian life:

> For you know what instructions we gave you through the Lord Jesus. For this is the will of God, your sanctification: that you abstain from fornication; that each one of you know how to control your own body [or "wife"?] in holiness and honor, not with lustful passion, like the Gentiles who do not know God; that no one wrong or exploit a brother or sister in this matter, because the Lord is an avenger in all these things, just as we have already told you beforehand. (4:3–6)

Paul gave orders less explicit than those he would deliver to the Corinthian Gentiles. He repeated something like the Holiness Code in Leviticus or the similar prophetic teaching about holiness, especially in regard to marital sex. His language might impress a Gentile hearer favorably if he or she happened to know contemporary Stoic teachers like Musonius Rufus (see below), many of whose ideas, and even expressions, Paul shared. But in Paul's view, violation of this kind of Jewish and Stoic ethic led to God's wrath upon the disobedient, as he would later insist to Roman Christians (Rom. 1:18–32). He reinforced his view with lists of virtues and vices.

Paul's third concern was with the fate of Christians who had already died. He uses purely Jewish imagery like that in the book of Daniel and other apocalypses. He claims to have a "word of the Lord" to explain that

> we who are alive, who are left until the coming of the Lord, will by no means precede those who have died. For the Lord himself, with a cry of command, with

> the archangel's call and with the sound of God's
> trumpet, will descend from heaven, and the dead in
> Christ will rise first. Then we who are alive, who are
> left, will be caught up in the clouds together with
> them to meet the Lord in the air; and so we will be
> with the Lord forever. (4:15–17)

Here we find vivid Jewish apocalyptic imagery, with archangels, trumpets, and even a specific location—the air—for meeting the Lord. It is not clear that Paul retained all these ideas as he got older and farther into the Gentile world, though the trumpet soon came back in 1 Corinthians 15:52. In any case, he brought this kind of language from Judaism to his early encounters with Gentiles.

Another letter to the Thessalonians deals with similar topics but so differently that critics have doubted that it is genuine. The author graphically describes God's impending judgment on persecutors "when the Lord Jesus is revealed from heaven with his mighty angels in flaming fire" (2 Thess. 1:7), but then insists that the day of the Lord has not already come, nor will it come before a schedule of apocalyptic events is followed through. There will be a "rebellion," presumably cosmic, with a "man of lawlessness" or "son of perdition" who not only will oppose pagan gods but also will "take his seat in the temple of God, declaring himself to be God" (2:1–4). Conceivably this is based on an episode in the reign of Caligula (A.D. 37–41), who ordered a statue of himself as Zeus set up in the temple at Jerusalem. Something or someone is now restraining the manifestation of this miracle-working "mystery of lawlessness" (2:7–10). Since the Thessalonians knew what caused the restraint (2:6), the author did not have to say what it was, though later Christians sometimes thought it was the Roman Empire, which Paul so strongly admired (Rom. 13:1–7). The end, on which he had so strongly insisted in his first letter, was not really at hand after all.

He therefore denounces idleness and calls attention to his

own example of working "night and day." He has told them, "Anyone unwilling to work should not eat" (3:10). His attitude may seem more Jewish than Greek, but such classifications are hard to apply, especially in his case. When he could say, "To the Jews I became as a Jew, in order to win Jews. To those under the law I became as one under the law (though I myself am not under the law) so that I might win those under the law" and "I have become all things to all people, that I might by all means save some" (1 Cor. 9:20–22), he obviously thought he was free of his ancestral religion. Yet his gospel to the Thessalonians, as he described it from Corinth, was Jewish, and he could not escape from Judaism any more than later Christianity could. He still speaks of the Jewish ancestors as his ancestors. On the other hand, many Greek authors, beginning with Hesiod, praise hard work just as much as Paul does.[2] As he wrote from Corinth to the Thessalonians he often had in mind considerations and even patterns related to Greek philosophy, as Malherbe has insisted.[3]

Paul at Athens

From Thessalonica, Christians brought Paul to Beroea and Athens (Acts 17:10–15). Acts depicts his preaching at Athens as deeply influenced by Hellenistic Judaism and even Greek popular philosophy, though the account owes almost everything to its author. Supposedly Paul was summoned before the court of the Areopagus at Athens on the very charge of religious innovation (preaching "foreign divinities") that had gotten Socrates killed much earlier.[4] Even Epicurean and Stoic philosophers take time to listen to him. He admits that the Athenians are indeed very religious and, more than that, have a basically true worship of God, though of an unknown God who needs to be proclaimed specifically to them (Acts 17:22–23). As Jerome insisted, the inscription must not have referred to "the [or "an"] unknown god" but "to the gods of

Asia and Europe and Africa, gods unknown and foreign."[5] Paul goes on to give them a semiphilosophical picture of a god of order not far from popular Stoic preaching. God is the creator and Lord of creation; he does not live in temples or need human offerings, "since he himself gives mortals life and breath and all things." He has made one humanity to form all nations and inhabit various regions of the earth, and he hopes that all will "grope for him and find him." Indeed, he is close to everyone: "In him we live and move and have our being" or, to quote a Greek poet, "For we too are his offspring." To be sure, the Stoic poet Aratus had meant that "we are the offspring of Zeus," but the Paul of Acts makes the verse his own, bypassing Zeus by following an older Jewish reinterpretation.[6]

Since we are this god's offspring, we ourselves, not works of art, are his best images (17:24–29). At the end of the address, Paul says that God has overlooked the times of ignorance, but now he has set a day for judgment "by a man whom he has appointed," confirming his choice by raising him from the dead (17:30–31). Here Paul finally leaves his cosmology and anthropology and turns back to his explicitly Christian message to the Thessalonians: "to wait for his Son from heaven, whom he raised from the dead—Jesus, who rescues us from the wrath that is coming" (1 Thess. 1:10). Apologetic usually proceeds in this way, moving from beliefs at least partly shared to those more controversial.

Naturally these last statements provoke dissent: "Some scoffed; but others said, 'We will hear you again about this.'" No evidence, however, suggests that they did hear him again. The passage as a whole suggests that Paul could recognize truths in religions not his own, neither Jewish nor Christian but related to God in their own way. How could he maintain his own traditions (*nostra nobis*, as Cicero says[7]) but broaden them and reach toward the adherents of other faiths? Paul did not solve the problem, but Acts presents him as moving beyond his own circles, and in his letter to the Romans he claims that God himself has disclosed "his eternal power and divine nature, invisible though they are, . . . through the things he has made" (Rom. 1:19–20). He thus recognizes with Hellenistic Jews like Philo of Alexandria that everyone can benefit, at least minimally, from God's self-revelation.

According to Acts, this was not Paul's first venture into apologetic preaching. Some years earlier he and Barnabas had been hailed as Hermes and Zeus at Lystra in Lycaonia, where both apostles were said to have insisted that they were mere mortals. They could work miracles but urged their hearers to "turn from these worthless things [idols and sacrifices] to the living God, who made the heaven and the earth and the sea and all that is in them" (Acts 14:15)—the other part of the gospel to the Thessalonians: "You turned to God from idols, to serve a living and true God" (1 Thess. 1:9). Next they stated, as in the Athens speech, "In past generations [God] allowed all the nations to follow their own ways," though he did not leave himself without witness because of gifts of rain and fruitful seasons that brought "food and gladness." Here the address breaks off because Paul "scarcely restrained the crowds from offering sacrifice to them" (Acts 14:15–18). The outline of this speech is close to the more highly developed Areopagus address. Presumably both follow a pattern of Hellenistic Jewish mission preaching like parts of the Wisdom of Solomon or, again, Philo. It may not be what Paul would have said. Perhaps it is what he should have said.

Paul at Corinth

From Athens, Paul proceeded, perhaps by land, to Corinth, where at first he argued in the Jewish synagogue (Acts 18:4)[8] but later moved next door to the house of a Gentile with the Latin names Titius Justus. He took with him "Crispus, the official of the synagogue, [who] became a believer in the Lord, together with all his household." Indeed, "many of the

Corinthians who heard Paul became believers and were baptized" during the year and a half Paul spent in Corinth (Acts
18:7–11). He himself says that his converts included sexual
transgressors and, more specifically, idolaters, adulterers, and
passive and active homosexuals; and finally, thieves, gluttons,
drunkards, abusive men, and robbers. Such persons, he insists,
are to be expelled from the community if they remain unrepentant (1 Cor. 6:9–13).[9] Were they ex-Jews? Presumably
they were not, but simply emerged during Paul's search for
Gentile converts.

Around the year 51, Paul himself was expelled from the
Jewish community and sailed from Corinth's eastern port of
Cenchreae (Acts 18:18),[10] then headed for Ephesus before
continuing on to Caesarea and traveling by land to Antioch in
Syria and returning to Ephesus (Acts 18:18–22; 19:1). During
his absence from Corinth, the community enjoyed the minis-
trations of a certain Apollos, a Jew from Alexandria who was
"well-versed in the scriptures." Though at Ephesus he "taught
accurately the things concerning Jesus, he knew only the baptism of John" until corrected by Paul's former companions
Priscilla and Aquila. Acts 19:1–6 indicates that his "baptism of
John" did not involve the Holy Spirit or speaking with tongues
or prophesying. Only baptism "in the name of the Lord Jesus"
could produce such manifestations. Troubles still existed
when Paul wrote 1 Corinthians, for he mentions Christians
who claimed to "belong to Apollos" and asks if they were "baptized in the name of Paul" or, by implication, Apollos (1 Cor.
1:12–23). Paul claims that while he "planted" at Corinth and
Apollos "watered," it was God who grew the crop of converts
(3:5–9). He also claims that he wanted Apollos to visit Corinth
again, but the time was not ripe. While he mentions Aquila
and Priscilla as sending greetings from Ephesus to the
Corinthians, he does not refer to greetings from Apollos. Perhaps Paul includes him as a member of "the churches of Asia"

(16:12, 19). We cannnot tell whether his language masks an abiding conflict or not.

A more serious disagreement, also reflected among the Corinthians, was with the apostle Cephas ("Peter" in Greek). Cephas was not only the earliest witness to the resurrection of Jesus (1 Cor. 15:3) but also an apostle of the highest rank, like the brothers of the Lord (9:5). Paul's insecurity regarding his own apostleship and his own vision of Jesus meant that he had to defend both by saying, "If I am not an apostle to others, at least I am to you; for you are the seal of my apostleship in the Lord" (9:2). He had to insist that Corinthian Christians could not claim to "belong to Cephas" (1:12). Paul did not tell the Corinthians about his controversy with Cephas (not evidently meaningful to them), but went into it rather fully in the first two chapters of Galatians.

These were some of the salient political, social, and personal factors in the background of 1 Corinthians. The letter cannot be understood apart from them, even if Paul's purpose was ultimately theological. Many of them confirm the picture of him in Acts, where he is proud of being a Roman citizen by birth.

2

Corinth: City and Church

In Paul's time, the famous Greek city of Athens was declining in importance when compared with the new and freshly Romanized city of Corinth. As J. A. O. Larsen observed, "Athens no longer could rival Corinth in commerce but owed her importance to her past, which helped her attract visitors and retain her prominence as a center of learning and art." The silver mines had given out, and while Attica still produced marble and olive oil, "except for some textiles and for objects of art produced at Athens there are few signs of industry of more than local importance."[1] What came down from the past included genealogies and great fortunes, notably the one confiscated under Vespasian from the aristocratic plotter Hipparchus but mysteriously recovered by his son Atticus from a house he owned.[2] Atticus twice asked the emperor Nerva if he could keep what he claimed to have found.[3] Once assured of imperial approval, he went on to philanthropy and even greater wealth, much of which he left to his son, the famous rhetorician Herodes Atticus.[4]

Trade and Wealth

Corinth was a more vulgar and commercial city than Athens, and the late versifier Alciphron, for example, preferred life at

13

Athens to luxury at Corinth, where the rich were shameless and the poor were wretched.[5] Like Carthage, Corinth was a Roman colony established by Julius Caesar shortly before his murder in 44 B.C. Both Corinth and Carthage stood on the ruins of cities that Roman armies had devastated in 146 B.C. They were almost unique in foundation, and served to advance the commercial interests of Rome and her unemployed poor. The geographer Strabo tells us that Corinth

> is called "wealthy" (*Iliad* 2.570) because of its commerce, since it is situated on the Isthmus and is master of two harbors,[6] one opening to Asia and the other to Italy, and it facilitates the exchange of goods from both, so far distant from each other. Just as in early times the Strait of Sicily was not easy to navigate, neither were the high seas and especially the sea beyond Malea, on account of the contrary winds: hence the proverb, "But when you double Malea forget your home." At any rate, it was a welcome alternative for the merchants both from Italy and from Asia to avoid the voyage to Malea and to land their cargoes here. The duties on what was exported by land to the Peloponnese and what was imported to it accrued to those who held the keys,[7] and this has always remained so. Still greater advantages were added to the Corinthians of later times, for the Isthmian games, celebrated there, customarily drew great crowds.[8]

This summary expands and confirms what Thucydides had said about the city's location and commercial life.[9]

The Roman politician Cicero is less helpful, since he moralizes in a traditionally Roman manner to explain Corinthian history, holding that Corinth (like Carthage) lost its traditions because as a seaport (unlike Rome) it imported foreign morals as well as merchandise. Lust for commerce and navigation, he says, drove out such old-fashioned and virtuous activities as agriculture and bearing arms. Pleasure took root through extravagant laziness, even though all the products of the world could be shipped in and local products sent out. Cicero's picture owes much to Polybius, who was present at the fall of Carthage in 146 B.C. and at Corinth after its fall.[10] It was Polybius who thought that agriculture and bearing arms, unlike vulgar commerce, were activities of pure and primitive states.[11] Later, Clement of Rome would blame deterioration in the Christian life of Corinth on its prosperity.

Not much reliable information about the city in Greco-Roman times comes from the other literary sources. Polybius charges that the *koinon* of the Achaeans at Corinth was made up of mere workmen and mechanics, and therefore was in a "driveling" state when dealing with the Romans in 147 B.C. Ernst Meyer takes this to mean that there was "a large industrial proletariat," but Polybius is simply writing out of prejudice against artisans, not as a sociologist.[12] Likewise, a "rhetorical exaggeration" by Seneca obviously does not apply to Corinth. The Roman rhetor asks plaintively, "Do you not see how in Achaea the foundations of the most famous cities have already crumbled to nothing, so that no trace is left to show that they had ever existed?" He goes on to show that he had Achaean earthquakes in mind, not economic decay.[13] Patriotic Greek orators inevitably continued to praise Corinth. The inept thirty-seventh *Oration* of Dio (actually written by Favorinus of Arles) calls it "the prow and poop [or 'stem and stern'] of Hellas" (in either case, a shipping image), while the *Isthmian Oration to Poseidon* by Aelius Aristides speaks of it as the seat of Roman justice and as wealthy, full of good things.[14] It had become the capital of the Roman province of Achaea.[15]

Roman Colonists

Who were the Roman colonists? Appian describes the men who were sent to colonize Carthage as primarily the poor of the city of Rome, those who needed employment and land and who were likely to cause trouble at home.[16] The colonists of

Corinth must have been much the same. Spawforth investi-
gates the coinage and epigraphy of Corinth from Augustus to
Nero and finds few veterans of Caesar's army among the
duumvirs, more of the ex-slaves of leading Roman families,
and still more businessmen and their ex-slaves. During the
reigns of Claudius and Nero, Corinthian commerce really
began to flourish. Before that, few old Greek families took part
in the city government, as Strabo already indicates, and few
veterans of the legions were involved.[17]

The key to Corinth's wealth was not manufacturing but
trade, and the trade depended on the Isthmus of Corinth, both
obstacle and incentive, with transfers of cargoes and passengers over land in both directions. Important passengers
included the poet Propertius, the exiled politician Flaccus, the
magician Apollonius, and Ovid, on his way east to exile in Pontus.[18] No author seems to have described the busy life of the
Corinthian ports, though we imagine it was like the Rome
praised by Aelius Aristides: "Arrivals and departures by sea
never cease, so that the wonder is, not that the harbor has
insufficient space for merchant vessels, but that even the sea
has enough, [if] it really does."[19]

Shipping

It is significant that the rulers of Corinth had tried to make
trade easy as early as the sixth century B.C., when the tyrant
Periander first built the important *diolkos* (portage) between
the Gulf of Corinth on the Ionian Sea and the Gulf of Aegina
on the Aegean. He intended to drag ships across at "the nar-
row part of the Isthmus"[20] and avoid the long voyage around
the southern Greek archipelago with its turbulent seas and
pirates. Oxen or men pulled the trolleys along the grooves of
the stone pavement,[21] mostly five meters wide though sometimes only three.[22] Pliny mentions vessels "prohibited by their
size from being carried across the Isthmus on carts."[23] The

channels cut in the pavement to guide the wheels of the movable wooden platform (the *holkos*) are, indeed, only 1.5 meters apart.[24] Several historians refer to the transit, naturally laying emphasis on exceptional naval episodes. Thucydides reports that in 412 B.C., the Spartans hauled their warships "over the Isthmus from the Corinthian Gulf to the sea on the side toward Athens"[25] in order to threaten the Athenians. Two centuries later, Philip V of Macedon dragged eight undecked ships and thirty light vessels across the Isthmus to avoid a Roman ally who was said to be a pirate, though twelve larger ships had to pass around Cape Malea.[26] In addition, a Corinthian inscription refers to a Roman fleet as passed along the *diolkos* in 102 B.C.,[27] and Cicero reveals the occasion for the transfer when he tells how M. Antonius visited Athens on his way to Cilicia against the Mediterranean pirates "because of difficulty in putting to sea."[28] In the winter of 31–30 B.C., Octavian used the *diolkos* to bring ships eastward from Italy against Antony and Cleopatra and finish the work begun at Actium (2 September 31).[29] The *diolkos* must have been used primarily for commerce, however, not for the military purposes emphasized in the literary evidence and still mentioned nearly a millennium later. In the ninth century, a Byzantine admiral slipped his fleet from Cenchreae westward by night to attack the Cretans, thus evading Saracen outpost boats off Cape Malea. The "barbarians" did not expect attack, perhaps because the *diolkos* was not normally in use.[30]

No early Christian author refers to the *diolkos* or, for that matter, to economic affairs at Corinth, though metaphorical machinery appears in Ignatius's *Letter to the Ephesians*. He tells them that they are "stones of the temple of the Father, prepared for the building of God the Father, lifted to the heights by the crane of Jesus Christ [the cross], using the Holy Spirit as a rope" (Ign. *Eph*. 9.1). His use of the image does not reflect any interest in real cranes. But few Corinthians can have been as "spiritual" as Ignatius.

Several ancient rulers intended to replace the *diolkos* by digging a broad and deep canal through the Isthmus.[31] The first was Periander himself,[32] followed by the Macedonian king Demetrius Poliorcetes,[33] the Roman dictator Julius Caesar (just before his murder),[34] the astute but unbalanced emperors Caligula and Nero, and the Athenian multimillionaire Herodes Atticus.[35] It was said that Nero, in Greece to win singing contests in A.D. 66–67 and deliver an "emancipation proclamation" at the Isthmian games, planned to rename the *Pelopon-nésos* (island of Pelops) the *Nerônos nésos* (island of Nero) in honor of himself.[36] Be that as it may, he was the only ruler after Periander to undertake real work on the project.[37] The third-century romancer Philostratus claims that the Cynic Demetrius encountered the Stoic Musonius Rufus at Corinth, digging for the canal on a chain gang,[38] while Pseudo-Lucian's *Nero* reports an imaginary discussion with Musonius on the canal's progress.[39] Vespasian, when still a general, sent six thousand prisoners from the Jewish war to dig on it, but halted the work after he became emperor.[40] The costs were too high. All other attempts failed before 1893. Shortly before the existing canal was begun, its chief engineer checked the remains of Nero's work and pointed out that it was not impromptu (as some ancient authors suggested) but had been planned for a long time. Nero's "perfectly straight" trenches, up to forty or fifty meters wide at both ends and ranging in depth from three to thirty meters, extended two thousand meters from the west and fifteen hundred from the east.[41]

Beyond questions of transport lies the matter of whether the Romans really destroyed the city in 146. The victorious Roman consul L. Mummius, who set up an inscription in the temple of Hercules Victor at Rome, claimed to have destroyed the city,[42] and Cicero, who saw the ruins, agreed with him.[43] (Evidence of habitation raises doubts about his claim.[44]) In any event, in Greece, Mummius "terminated democracies and established governments based on property qualifications," also imposing tribute on Greece[45] and thus readying the city for Roman rule. None of the "old Corinthians" lived there after 146,[46] for it was not refounded for a century, and then as a Roman colony it became the capital of Achaea. The so-called "veterans of Caesar's army" were mostly ex-slaves who removed ruins, dug into graves, and filled Rome with "Corinthian corpses," as the looted art was known.[47] How many colonists were there? Appian writes of Carthage, "I have ascertained that Augustus sent 3000 colonists from Rome and the rest [another 3000?] from the environs."[48] Presumably the figures for Corinth were similar, though of course they refer only to the very foundation of the new city. As the Romans rebuilt Corinth, they did not follow the old street lines but laid it out Roman style, with grid patterns like those in American cities.[49] Saffrey notes that twenty-two *duoviri* (the highest magistrates) of the next century bore Latin names, as against only nine Greek, while New Testament texts referring to Corinth give six Latin names to four Greek.[50] The official language of the city was now Latin, though as Larsen observed, "While the coins bear Latin legends, both Latin and Greek were used in inscriptions."[51] The province of Achaea was classified as senatorial in 27 B.C., imperial in A.D. 15, and senatorial again in A.D. 44.[52] All this evidence shows that the new Corinth was essentially a Roman city, even though the extant letters of Paul, Clement of Rome, and Dionysius of Corinth show that the ordinary language of those Corinthians who became Christians continued to be Greek. This evidence is inadequate to show what the language of people more closely related to business was.

Strabo tells us that "the city of the Corinthians was always great and rich, well provided with men skilled in political affairs and craftsmen's arts both graphic and plastic," while its lands were unsuited to agriculture.[53] Corinthian ceramics and Corinthian bronzes confirm Strabo's statement about arts and crafts, while Pliny and Petronius show how valuable

Corinthian bronzes were.[54] Though Augustus was a famous collector of these bronzes, the commercial center grew prosperous especially under Claudius and Nero.[55] Plutarch refers to moneylenders and businessmen at Corinth, Patrae, and Athens.[56] It was an international city, with gladiatorial fights as well as bears and leopards in the theater.[57] People said that Athens imitated Corinth when it too began to keep gladiators.[58]

Religion

Religious cults included those of Egypt as well as Greece and Rome. Among Corinth's many temples were several on the mountain of Acrocorinth dedicated to the Egyptian Isis, whose festival there Apuleius describes.[59] At the top of the mountain stood a small temple of Aphrodite,[60] said to have owned a thousand prostitutes, presumably as part of the endowment. The verb *korinthiazesthai* (to "Corinthize")[61] and the saying, "Not everybody gets to sail to Corinth"[62] prove nothing about Corinthian reality, however, any more than a character in Plato's *Republic* who intimates that to keep a "Corinthian girl" is bad for a man's health.[63] The ruins of the citadel, razed much later, naturally do not hint at such activities. Perhaps the scene was livelier two thousand years ago, though Strabo, writing in the late first century B.C., claimed that the citadel had not been inhabited since 146.[64] Alciphron, who preferred Athenians, insisted that the Corinthians were "people ungracious and unblessed by Aphrodite."[65]

According to the orator Dio Chrysostom in the reign of Domitian, Diogenes the Cynic lived in Corinth because he was looking for fools there amid the "multitudes gathered on account of the harbors and the prostitutes."[66] He was buried beside the gate that led to the Isthmus, though his tomb, apparently seen by Pausanias in the second century, is now lost. In a nearby gymnasium, Diogenes encountered Alexander the Great and asked him not to stand in his sunshine. Diogenes Laertius says that the Corinthians later inscribed bronze statues of him thus: "Even bronze ages with time, but all eternity will not destroy your fame, Diogenes; since you alone showed mortals the glory of self-sufficiency and the easiest path of life."[67] Later we shall consider Corinthian acquaintance with ideas disseminated by the Cynic Demetrius and the Stoic Musonius.

3

Religion and Politics

First Corinthians presents Paul's political and religious views in opposition to Corinthian leaders and thus permits some practical conclusions about the political-philosophical shape of the church there.[1] To assess these political ideas, we shall compare them with Aristotle's *Politics*, even though Paul never read a line of this work. Aristotle was certainly not a popular philosopher in the Roman world, and Paul may not even have known (or cared) who he was.[2] Since, however, the Paul of Acts 21:39 proudly declares himself "a citizen of an important city," we should expect him to have some understanding of urban life and government and perhaps to hold views not unlike Aristotle's.[3]

The main point of 1 Corinthians appears toward the beginning (1:10) and is repeated at the very end (16:15–18). At the beginning, Paul asks the Corinthians "that all of you be in agreement, and that there be no divisions among you, but that you be united in the same mind and the same purpose." Scholars have provided excellent parallels from Greek historians but have not always recognized how much the Corinthians' conflicts resembled those within Greek city-states as described by ancient historians and how close Paul's concern for peace and

23

harmony was to that of politicians, rhetoricians, and philosophers.[4] The basic political ideas expressed by Paul are "rebellion" and "concord." His goal is much the same as the
harmony advocated in *1 Clement* and by Plutarch and many
other Greek authors. So the letter was understood, at least in
part, by John Chrysostom in the fourth century.[5] Some modern critics have taken the letter in the same way.[6]

To make this point, we must neglect many details and the
theological grounding that differentiates Paul from an ordinary Greek politician. His picture of the end of the world does
make everything relative, at least in theory. Perhaps it even
makes him think of equal rights for wife and husband (1 Cor.
7:2–4). The idea is more fully expressed without eschatology
by the Stoic Musonius Rufus, however (see below), and the
picture of Onesimus as "more than a slave, a beloved brother"
(Philemon 16) does not seem based on either egalitarian or
end-of-the-world ideas.

Paul's basic attitude is conservative. His worldview is hierarchical and, in the local church, monarchical.[7] By the time of
Ignatius, the bishop will be the local monarch, but for Paul it
is the apostle who rules. God himself set apostles first in the
church, locally as well as universally (1 Cor. 12:28), and Paul
is the one apostle to the Corinthians (9:2).

Philo and Josephus

Such political analysis would not have surprised a Hellenistic
Jew in Paul's time. Both Philo and Josephus were deeply concerned with politics and both emphasized hierarchies. The
Jewish philosopher Philo liked the mixed constitution (monarchical, aristocratic, democratic) that Romans claimed to possess.[8] He favored conservative aristocracy with one-man rule.
He was rather vehement about the evils of rule by the mob
under one vote per man and contrasted it with the blessings of
parental authority. This ideal arrangement "is not obtained by

lot or vote as it is in the cities, where it may be alleged that the lot is due to a blunder of fortune in which reason has no place, and the voting to the impetuosity of the mob, always so reckless and lacking circumspection."[9] (Like Philo, the later Christian Clement of Alexandria disliked mob rule and said so.[10]) The retired Jewish general Josephus occasionally favored democracy but reserved his highest praise for aristocracy, in its priestly form equivalent to the rule of God. Monarchy, according to his *Antiquities*, too easily turns into tyranny. The aristocracy of the high priests is, of course, what he knew as a youth in Judea.[11] In a later apologetic work, he states that while other peoples had monarchies, oligarchies, or the rule of the masses, "our lawgiver gave his constitution the form of what—if a forced expression be permitted—may be termed a 'theocracy,' ascribing all sovereignty and authority to God."[12] Josephus was the first to use the word "theocracy," but Paul would have been glad to use it had he known it. This theocracy was in fact the rule of the best, chosen by God for his purposes. Among the Jews, the best were the high priests. Among the Christians, they were the apostles and those chosen by the apostles to rule the communities.

Divisions at Corinth

Paul describes Corinthian divisions thus: "Each of you says, 'I belong to Paul,' or 'I belong to Apollos,' or 'I belong to Cephas,' or 'I belong to Christ'" (1:12). Is Paul speaking for himself as belonging to Christ? A parallel expression is inscribed on a bronze vase of the sixth century B.C. from Corinth (presumably a votive offering): "I belong to Aphrodite." It would be significant, however, only if the inscription were a reflection of some conflict in the cult rather than a simple dedication to the goddess.

At one point, Paul accommodates himself to the Corinthian situation and says that "there have to be factions among you, for only so will it become clear who among you are genuine" (11:19). The early Christian exegetes Theodoret and John Chrysostom point out that these "factions" are related not to doctrinal squabbles but to social divisions. Chrysostom mentions rich and poor. The second-century letter writer Alciphron insists that at Corinth the rich were contemptible and the poor were wretched.[13] Presumably this was a political judgment rather than a scientific one.

Paul's admission that divisions have a useful function faintly resembles philosophers' attacks on dogmatism,[14] but it is closer to Aristotle's claim in the *Rhetoric* that "the orator ought to be able to prove opposites . . . so that the real state of the case may not escape us."[15] Truth comes dialectically, that is, in dialogue. Successful politicians are always opposed to "acrimony and discord," for a badly divided society can succumb to struggles either internal or external.[16] Thucydides has the Spartans say to the Athenians that "if we and you say the same thing [i.e., come to agreement], the rest of the Hellenic world will pay us the greatest honor." Not surprisingly, the proponents of this kind of unity had an oligarchic, not a democratic, government.[17] Some centuries later, Plutarch discussed in *Precepts of Statecraft* how the upperclass rulers of a city are to govern it: "You must take care that they [the people] are never discordant; this is the greatest and noblest feature of the art of politics." Indeed, the best sign of the happiness of a city is "the quietness and tranquility of the people." There is, to be sure, freedom, but in Plutarch's time under Roman rule "the peoples have as great a share of freedom as the rulers grant them, and more might not be better."[18] It thus becomes clear that concord is more important than liberty.

Paul, like Plutarch, has little use for promoters of strife (1:11), divisions (11:18), or sectarianism (11:19). Against these he appeals to logic and empirical evidence. When he came to Corinth he did not employ "plausible words of wisdom." Instead, his gospel was demonstrated by Spirit and divine power (2:4). The idea of demonstration "not by persuasive words but clear demonstrations" appears again in Galen, who appeals to anatomical observation for proof.[19] Paul thus insists on the importance of the rational and the empirical. He is not a professional writer, however. Like the later "preachers" of popular philosophy, his preliminary teaching was oral, not written. Margarethe Billerbeck names Demetrius, Musonius, and Epictetus as speakers, not writers.[20] I add Peregrinus Proteus and Paul, even though there was controversy among the Corinthians over Paul's letter writing and speaking (2 Cor. 10:10–11).

Wise, Well Born, Noble

In the Corinthian community, Paul notes the presence of not many wise, not many powerful, not many noble (*eugeneis*; 1:26). Many scholars have pointed out that while such terms have philosophical overtones, they reflect political-social realities. But we remain in the dark as to what a few, most, or all Corinthians had in mind. What could they have said? Did they say, "We are wise, powerful, noble," on the basis of a small group's spiritual attainments? Or did they say, "All of us are wise, powerful, noble," and therefore we can run our community's affairs without outside interference, even if apostolic? Or could they even have claimed with the Cynic Diogenes that good birth (*eugeneia*), fame, and all such distinctions were "adornments of vice"?[21] Is Paul's real target an opposition to hierarchy?

We shall see other hints that this may be the case. Aristotle points out that in a democracy there are few rich people and many poor ones, though all share in liberty.[22] He criticizes democratic government. Since its foundation is liberty, there are no permanent rulers or ruled but equal sharers of power.[23] The operations of daily life are governed by majority decisions and the ways of life "as each one chooses." The result is that you have "election of officials by all from all; government of each by all, and of all by each in turn; . . . judicial functions to be exercised by all citizens, that is by persons selected from all, and on all matters, or on most and the greatest and most important, for instance the audit of official accounts," and so on. At the end of this sensible discussion, Aristotle remarks that "inasmuch as oligarchy is defined by birth, wealth, and education [think of "wise, powerful, noble"], "the democratic qualifications are thought to be the opposite of these, low birth, poverty, vulgarity."[24] Is something like this in Paul's mind? Is he using a democratic slogan against democratic Corinthians, especially when he says that God chose the ignoble of the world and the "nothings," the "nonexistent," in order to destroy the existent (1:28)? Still further, how are these "existent" people related to the "existent" powers ordained by God according to Romans 13:1?

Or does Paul use a slogan from popular philosophy against his opponents in the first three chapters of the letter? The ideal Stoic wise man was supposedly the only one to be wise, well born, and powerful. Perhaps politics could fuse with Cynic-Stoic popular philosophy to give the Corinthians a high opinion of themselves. Obviously they could have learned such philosophy from the migrant philosophers of their time. If Paul originally came from Tarsus (uncertain, though emphasized in Acts 21:39), he could have been influenced by the schools of philosophy and rhetoric there.[25] The famous Stoic Athenodorus had left Tarsus to become head of the library at Pergamum. A Pergamene author notes that he deleted passages in Zeno's works of which the Stoic school had come to disapprove. Later, however, he was detected and endangered by non-Stoics or, at least, critics of Zeno.[26] Plutarch says that he had "resisted all friendships with governors and kings" (was he antimonarchical or mindful of Plato's dealings with the tyrant of Syracuse?) but in old age was visited by Cato the Younger, who took him back to Rome as a permanent guest.[27] This mixture of philosophy and politics reminds us of Corinth and of Paul himself, though it hardly helps explain Paul's language.

As Paul's letter progresses, he discusses the political topics Aristotle mentions. He is aware that in his ideal oligarchy there can be discord among the leaders. This is why he insists on the joint operation of himself and Apollos, both under God (3:9).[28] It is why he picks the model of the architect, himself, who begins the building of the church. Others have to build on the same foundation (3:10), that is, according to the same plan. "An architect chooses subordinates and workmen who will not spoil his work but will best labor together."[29]

It is true that Paul agrees with the Corinthians, that everything belongs to (all of) them (3:20–23). Their notion is obviously borrowed from the Cynic-Stoic picture of the ideal wise man to whom everything belongs,[30] discussed at length by Seneca in his seventh book, *On Benefits*. Like Seneca, they may well postulate that everything belongs to the gods[31] or, on a Jewish or Christian basis, to God (cf. 1 Chron. 29:11, "All things come of thee"). Then, since friends hold everything in common and the wise (themselves) are the friends of the gods or of God, everything belongs to the wise.[32] This arrangement obviously sets the wise at the divine level. Paul's arrangement and counterstatement reverts to hierarchy. Everything does belong to you, "and you belong to Christ, and Christ belongs to God" (3:21–23). This arrangement resembles 1 Corinthians 11:3: "Christ is the head of every man, and the husband is the head of his wife, and God is the head of Christ." (The wife thus belongs to her husband as he belongs to Christ and Christ to God.)

In chapter 4, Paul suggests that the Corinthians are mistakenly puffed up with pride. (Diogenes had attacked those who were "puffed up" over fame and wealth.[33]) "Already you have all you want! Already you have become rich! Quite apart from us you have become kings! Indeed, I wish that you had become kings, so that we might be kings with you!" (4:8). This continues the allusion to the Cynic-Stoic wise man ideal, to which he will return in 9:1 ("Am I not free?"). The wise man was the only free man; he was rich, and he was a king.[34] God's kingdom will belong to Corinthian Christians, but they have wrongly antedated its joys. A beatitude of Jesus—the possible source of Paul's accusation that the Corinthians have all they want—refers to being "filled" in the future (Luke 6:21, cf. Matt. 5:6), not the present.

Sufferings

Paul contrasts his real sufferings for the gospel with the spurious claims the Corinthians make (4:9–13). When he says that like other apostles he is condemned to die as a theater spectacle, he probably has something like gladiators in mind: "To the present hour we are hungry and thirsty, we are poorly clothed and beaten and homeless, and we grow weary from the work of our own hands" (4:11–12). In 2 Corinthians, Paul lists more of his sufferings, this time contrasted with claims by "pseudo-apostles," as

> far greater labors, far more imprisonments, with countless floggings, and often near death. Five times I have received from the Jews the forty lashes minus one. Three times I was beaten with rods. Once I received a stoning. Three times I was shipwrecked; for a night and a day I was adrift at sea; on frequent journeys, in danger from rivers, danger from bandits, danger from my own people, danger from Gentiles, danger in the city, danger in the wilderness, danger at sea, danger from false brothers and sisters; in toil and hardship, through many a sleepless night, hungry and thirsty, often without food, cold and naked. (11:23–27; cf. 6:4–10; 12:10)[35]

This longer list of sufferings for the gospel resembles in form, though not in content, the achievement lists for Greek

and Roman generals and kings, especially the *Res gestae* of the
emperor Augustus. Anton Fridrichsen drew attention to Hellenistic parallels in inscriptions and Plutarch's *Lives*, with lists
of achievements by kings and generals.[36] He also noted the
lists of sufferings for love in the romances of Chariton and
Achilles Tatius.[37] As in the novel of Chariton, Paul concen-
trated on what had happened to him. "Whenever I am weak,
then I am strong" (12:10). Indeed, his expressions resemble an
imaginary plaint of the heroine Leucippe in Achilles Tatius:

> You know what I have suffered for you, but I must
> remind you now. For you I left my mother and
> became a wanderer; for you I suffered shipwreck and
> was taken by pirates; for you I became a sacrificial vic-
> tim and an offering and even suffered death twice; for
> you I was sold and bound with a chain and carried a
> hoe and dug the ground and was beaten. . . . Through
> all these trials I kept on to the end.[38]

The similarity of this claim to Paul's is obvious, though similar form or even content obviously does not mean that Paul's
motivation was the same as Leucippe's.

Court Cases

Court cases come up in 1 Corinthians 6 (for 5:3–5, 13 see
chapter 8), where as usual the situation is not altogether clear.
Some Christians have engaged in civil suits against others.
Paul advises against lawsuits of any kind, though he holds that
Christians themselves are competent to try "trivial cases."
Does this refer to something like Aristotle's notion of small
claims courts that gave judgments of one drachma or five?[39]
In any event, the Corinthians should not seat as judges "those
who have no standing in the church"; instead, there should be
a (single) "wise" judge (6:2, 4). Rostovtzeff described the "corruption and inefficiency of regular city lawcourts" in the second century B.C.[40] (An inscription expresses the thanks of Elis

to visiting judges from Corinth—not small claims, of course.[41]) These courts were Hellenistic, possibly more honest under the Roman Empire, though Apuleius denounces second-century lawyers at Corinth as "vultures in togas" and says that "all our judges sell their judgments for money."[42] In any event, Paul did not want Christian conflicts aired before them. It would be better to suffer a loss than go to court (6:7). This sentiment is not uniquely Christian, as excellent parallels in Hellenistic moralists show.[43] And it is political, not especially religious. Who is going to suffer the loss? Perhaps a comment in chapter 4 helps explain the situation. Paul calls himself a "steward of God's mysteries" (cf. 9:17), notes that a qualified steward must be trustworthy, and immediately adds, "It is a very small thing that I should be judged by you or by any human court. I do not even judge myself. I am not aware of anything against myself, but I am not thereby acquitted. It is the Lord who judges me" (4:1–4). We might infer that Paul has wrongly been suspected of inadequate accounting, that he refuses to have his accounts audited, that it is God who will audit.[44] This is a far cry from the Athenian democratic auditing described by Aristotle. But it fits in with Paul's insistence upon divine authority, not to be questioned by the Corinthian congregation. Are some Corinthians threatening to sue him in the courts of Corinth? He refuses to accept their judgment or that of any human court.

Corinthian Knowledge

At the end of the chapter, Paul deals with some slogans of the Corinthians (6:12–20). Like other exponents of the Greco-Roman diatribe, Paul imitates actual speech when he presents his arguments to the Corinthians. For example, he introduces rhetorical questions with the formula, "Do you not know that." This feature occurs ten times in 1 Corinthians but only once elsewhere in Paul's letters, in Romans 6:16 (written at Corinth) where he asks, "Do you not know that . . . you are

slaves of the one whom you obey?" Presumably this knowledge was obvious, but other "knowns" included some rather
abstruse theological matters. We shall examine later the content of their teaching and Paul's on sex (chapter 9). Now we
look at the form of their statements and his.

The Corinthians were supposed to know (1) that they were
a temple of God (3:16), (2) that a little yeast leavens the whole
lump (5:6—proverbial wisdom?), (3) that the saints will judge
the world (6:2), (4) that the saints will judge angels (6:3), and (5)
that the unjust will not inherit the kingdom of God (6:9).
These examples have to do chiefly with Christian teaching
about the coming reign of God and his saints, on which Paul
lays emphasis in 1 Corinthians 15. It was set forth earlier in the
Jewish book of Daniel (7:22). Paul also deals with teaching (6)
about the Corinthians' members as members of Christ (6:15)
and (7) the notion that a man who unites with a prostitute is
one with her in body, which is proved by Genesis 2:24 (6:16).
He repeats the axiom (8) that the body is a temple of the Holy
Spirit (6:19; cf. 3:16) but seems to rely on general information
for the notions (9) that men who perform temple rites get their
food from the temple (9:13, differently in 10:18) and (10) that
of those who run in the stadium only one receives the prize
(9:24). Much of what they are supposed to know, in other
words, comes from their shared Greco-Roman, that is,
Corinthian, culture.

Or could we interpret further? Since so much of his "do you
not know" material comes from 1 Corinthians 6, in which he
repeatedly quotes and corrects Corinthian claims, may he not
be using their formula against them as well? Examples of
things corrected include their slogan, "All things are lawful for
me" and their analogy "Food is meant for the stomach and the
stomach for food" (6:12–13). He vehemently rejects their
inference that "the body is for sex and sex for the body," insisting that God will destroy both food and stomach. Certainly
they could have asked, "Do you not know . . . ?"—the formula
he uses against them in 6:15: "Do you not know that your bod-

ies are members of Christ?" We shall consider his use of the
Cynic-Stoic appeal to "nature" (11:14) later in this chapter. In
10:23–24 he repeats their slogan, "All things are lawful." He
does not reject it but this time corrects it by insisting on what
is "profitable" (an expression from the Stoics) and "edifying"
(from the Old Testament).

Marriage and Separation

The center of Paul's subsequent discussion of marriage, separation, and remarriage in chapters 5–7 lies in 7:17–24, with the
essentially conservative counsel, "Stay as you are" or "Don't
make waves." There is a verbal parallel in Ovid's *Fasti*: "Stay
where you have been placed."[45] In Paul's view, this maxim
applies to both marriage and slavery, and he describes the two
in similar terms.

His discussion of life in marriage is political as well as sexual (see chapter 9). In this regard he agrees with Aristotle, who
insists that a lawgiver must "pay attention to the union of the
sexes and settle when and in what condition a couple should
practise matrimonial intercourse."[46] Stoic moralists also
treated marriage as a political question. For Paul and some
Corinthians, "It is well for a man not to touch a woman" (7:1).
But he partly shares a more "natural" (later Stoic) ethical view,
sexually egalitarian, which he thinks can justify marital intercourse because of the prevalence of "fornication."

A passage toward the end of the chapter (7:29–31) is eschatological in form but not in content. It begins with Paul's
solemn declaration, "I mean, brothers and sisters, the
appointed time has grown short," and ends with "the present
form of this world is passing away." He instructs the Corinthians that "those who have wives be as though they had none,
and those who mourn as though they were not mourning, and
those who rejoice as though they were not rejoicing, and those
who buy as though they had no possessions, and those who

deal with the world as though they had no dealings with it."
The basic content of this list, apart from eschatology, resembles Cynic teaching, except that what for Paul is hypothetical
("as though") is actual for Diogenes. He praised "those going
to marry who did not marry, to sail who did not sail, to enter
politics who did not enter politics, to raise children who did
not raise children, those preparing to live with tyrants who did
not approach them."[47] Here it is Paul who stands close to
Cynic teachings, not the Corinthians.

Taxation

It should be noted here that in Romans, written from Corinth,
Paul insists on the payment of taxes to all governmental bodies, imperial as well as local (Rom. 13:6–7). The Naassene
Gnostics, indeed, found taxes indicated in 1 Corinthians.
When Jesus said, "the tax collectors and the prostitutes are
going into the kingdom of God ahead of you" (Matt. 21:31),
the "tax collectors" are those who receive the taxes (*telé*) of the
ages and we are the tax collectors "to whom the taxes [*telé*] of
the ages have come" (1 Cor. 10:11)—less verbally, "upon
whom the ends of the ages have come."[48] Naturally this exegesis is absurd, but at Corinth as elsewhere Paul was aware of
taxes. In Romans he tells his readers that tax collectors are the
ministers of God, attending to tax collection. Therefore,
Christians must pay to all their due, tribute (*phoroi* = *tributum*,
based on the census) to whom tribute is due, revenue (*telé*, usually customs duties[49]) to whom revenue is due, as well as
respect and honor (13:6–7). Such customs duties were especially important for Corinth.

Diet and Meals

Another practical concern dominates the discussion in 1 Corinthians 8–10. Some Christians realize that they are free from

the Jewish law and can eat anything they like. Others still consider problematic the meats that are sacrificed to pagan gods and then sold in the meat market. One could easily say that each should do what he or she prefers. But the sensitivity of those who worry about sacrifices has made difficulties for the bolder spirits, who apparently insist on their right to eat sacrificed meats even in pagan temples, where a "weak" believer may sight the "knowing" Christian, follow that person's example, and harm his own conscience (8:10). Two chapters later, however, Paul says that a Christian is to eat anything sold in the meat market (10:25), and if an unbeliever invites a Christian to dinner and he chooses to accept, he is to eat everything set before him, unless someone tells him that the meat has been offered in sacrifice (10:27–28). Awareness of the offering means that conscience is involved.

Lietzmann and many others have quoted papyrus notes inviting guests to meals at various temples or private houses.[50] The most widely cited is this: "Chaeremon invites you to dine at the banquet of the Lord Sarapis in the Sarapeum tomorrow, the 15th, beginning at the 9th hour."[51] Probably no religious ceremony was connected with such a meal (note that P Oxy 3.523 is an invitation "to dine with him at the banquet of the Lord Sarapis in the home of Claudius Sarapion"), but the reference to "the Lord Sarapis," not "the Lord Jesus," might cause difficulties for "weak" Christians. Paul explains that while there are many "so-called" gods and lords in the world, for Christians there is only one God and one Lord (1 Cor. 8:6).

Rights and Freedom

Paul offers a series of solutions that do not solve the problem but encourage thought and consideration. Concerned with unity in the Corinthian church, he wants its members to share his concern. He urges them to be considerate of others, to keep in mind what builds up the community rather than their own liberty. As in chapter 7, there is a central section that con-stitutes the heart of Paul's political message. In chapters 8—10 it is chapter 9, where he insists on the importance of not fully exercising his rights. It is his "defense" against critics. Though he argues at length for the right to be supported by his congregations (9:3–14), he does not exercise it (vv. 15–18).[52] In the *Nicomachean Ethics*, Aristotle passes from an analysis of *homonoia* (concord) to discuss "the base, incapable of concord, since they try to get more than their share of advantages" and finally argues that "the virtuous man will surrender wealth and power and all the goods that men struggle to win, if he can secure nobility for himself."[53] This is the way Paul speaks in this chapter.

Though like the Corinthians he is "free from all," Paul has become "a slave to all" in order that he "might win more of them." He became, for example, "as a Jew, in order to win Jews." Indeed, he became "all things to all people, that I might by all means save some. I do it all for the sake of the gospel, so that I may share in its blessings" (9:19–23). As Henry Chad-wick saw many years ago, "it is possible, though not demon-strable, that here he is actually quoting from his adversaries. It would be quite consistent with his usual practice if he were doing so, and in the Corinthian letters Paul seems especially inclined to take the charges of his opponents and quote them back in an ironic tone."[54]

After explaining that he does not insist on his rights, he ends by referring to life as a race to receive an imperishable wreath, contrasted with the perishable, indeed withered, wreath of the Isthmian games.[55] He himself does not "run aimlessly, nor do I box as though beating the air; but I punish my body and enslave it, so that after proclaiming to others I myself should not be disqualified."[56] His pattern is political as once more he gives advice, not legislation, to his converts.

In the tenth chapter (still on diet), such ideas recur: "Do not seek your own advantage, but that of the other" (10:24, cf. 10:33; 13:5). So in the *Nicomachean Ethics*, Aristotle recalls that "we are told that we ought to wish our friend well for his own sake"; this indeed is what a king does, not a tyrant.[57] And in the *Politics*: "To bestow favors and assistance on friends or visitors or companions is a great pleasure, and a condition of this is the private ownership of property."[58] Paul goes on to generalize about idolatry and resisting temptation: "No testing has overtaken you that is not common to everyone" (10:13). Marcus Aurelius makes a similar point: "Nothing happens to anyone that it is not his nature to bear. Others have the same experience . . . but stand firm and are not harmed."[59]

Women in Church

Chapter 11 begins with disorders in public meetings, related to the liberty of women in the church who pray or prophesy with their heads uncovered. Paul is firmly opposed to this practice because, in his opinion, supported by at least six dubious arguments, women should be subject to men. One such argument is found in verse 14: "Does not nature itself teach you that if a man wears long hair, it is degrading to him?" In fact, nature teaches nothing of the sort.

A thoughtful discussion by Musonius Rufus cites Zeno (SVF 1.243) "that it is quite as natural to cut the hair as it is to grow it long, in order not to be burdened by it nor hampered for any activity."[60] In his *Encomium on Hair*, Dio Chrysostom insists that attractive men have long hair.[61] Epictetus claims simply that it is the beard that distinguishes men from women.[62] Obviously there was no agreement on what nature taught. If Paul took over diatribe rhetoric from his opponents, he may not have understood just what their appeal to "nature" involved.

Perhaps Paul was relying on local (orientalizing) custom. In Tarsus, where he may have been born, it was customary for women to "have their faces covered as they walk."[63] But his basic point is stated by Aristotle, who tells us that "freedom for women is harmful both for the purpose of the constitution and for the happiness of the state." He adds that in the final and worst form of democracy there is "gynocracy," rule by women, in the homes.[64] Thus, while in chapter 11 Paul insists on women's veils as tokens of submissiveness, in chapter 14 he may be ready to demand their absolute silence.[65] Married women "are not permitted to speak"[66] but should be subordinate, as even the law says; apparently he has in mind a verse (Gen. 3:16) about the wickedness of Eve: "If there is anything they desire to know, let them ask their husbands at home. For it is shameful for a woman to speak in church" (14:34–35).[67] The same prejudice appears in Plutarch, who firmly advocates women's silence and the husband as teacher.[68] (The teaching of Musonius is more radical.[69]) Paul, or a Paulinist, offers conservative behavior as the Corinthians' model.

Men in Church

He returns to divisions and factions in the latter part of chapter 11 and discusses what happens at the Lord's Supper when some are hungry and others get drunk. Those who are drunk "show contempt for the church of God and humiliate those who have nothing" (11:22). Obviously this is not an ideological division but a tangible, factual one related to the possession of more or less property. Indeed, apparently some of the better-off Corinthian Christians are sick and some have died (11:30). The rich are to wait for the poor when they eat this supper (11:33), just as in the Greek city all were to share in the common meals.[70]

Chapter 12 deals with spiritual gifts, significantly with political unity within the body politic of Christ. The chapter opens with insistence that no one speaking in the Spirit can say "Let Jesus be cursed," just as no one can say "Jesus is Lord" except by the Holy Spirit (12:3). This resembles the political conflict between Jews and Romans over whether God was "the only and just master of men" and whether Romans were better than Jews, who considered God their only master. Romans tortured radical Jews so that they would acknowledge "Caesar as master."[71] Paul transfers the authority to Christ. He does not necessarily know anyone who has cursed Jesus.

The Church As Body

For some centuries, speakers and writers on politics had been using the analogy of the human body in regard to the workings of the state. It appeared among Romans during a political crisis when a patrician leader used the body figure to answer the charge that patricians did nothing but consume. He thus claimed that the stomach was essential for digestion and the transmission of blood to the various parts.[72] The comparison was still common in Paul's time, when people spoke of the body even without special reference to the stomach, noting rivalries between such members as hands and feet, eyes and hands (this example comes from Seneca[73]). Paul treats the subject in the same way, without defending patricians. He tells of feet versus hands, ears versus eyes, eyes versus hands, head versus feet. He also refers vaguely to the less honorable or less presentable parts, whether sexual or digestive, but apparently they are not in conflict with the rest as the stomach was in the fable of Menenius Agrippa.[74] Paul is primarily concerned with preventing divisions, not classifying parts. He wants mutual concern and sympathy in the Christian body politic (12:25–26).[75]

In Paul's version, this body politic becomes the body of Christ (12:12, 18, 24), and it is God who has "adjusted" the body against discord (12:24–25). A speech ascribed to Alcibiades had set the adjustment on a more "natural" basis: "Youth and age cannot do anything without each other, but the simple, the mediocre, and the very subtle, when adjusted together, will have most strength." "Alcibiades" claimed his opponent was creating divisions by "setting at variance."[76] The body imagery even appears in a Gnostic treatise from Nag Hammadi, *Interpretation of Knowledge* (11.1).[77]

Love

After the body (chap. 12) and before a more detailed discussion of particular spiritual gifts (chap. 14), Paul provides a more general theoretical but also politically oriented chapter, in which the essential practical description appears in a few verses in the middle (13:4–7), between an introduction on the necessity of love (vv. 1–3)[78] and a conclusion on the permanence of love (vv. 8–13). The point is simple: Love is "the tie that binds" everything together in the community and prevents discord and division. "Love is patient; love is kind; love is not envious or boastful or arrogant or rude. It does not insist on its own way; it is not irritable or resentful; it does not rejoice in wrongdoing, but rejoices in the truth. It bears all things, believes all things, hopes all things, endures all things" (vv. 4–7).

Though Paul insists on love of neighbor, he certainly does not exclude love of self. Indeed, the commandment in Leviticus and in the teaching of Jesus would seem to imply its necessity.[79] Aristotle points out that "the feeling of love toward oneself that each one has is not purposeless but a natural instinct." "Selfishness (*philauton*)," he adds, "is justly blamed; it means not to love oneself but to love oneself more than one ought."[80] Similarly, Augustine says that in God's two precepts man finds three objects of love: God, himself, and his neighbor.[81]

While the "hope" of verse 13 momentarily points toward Christian eschatology, the rest of the passage indicates a way of life in accord with Greek political ideals already intimated in the letter thus far, though it is less pointedly political than *1 Clement* 49:5: "Love contains no division, love does not rebel, love does everything in harmony." Similarly, the Greek rhetorician Maximus begins his rhetorical praise of Eros with the political aspects of love, goes on to the personal powers it conveys, and ends with praise of its universal supremacy. Presumably Paul's own rhetorical model was something like that.[82] The political content of his thought is paralleled in the *Nicomachean Ethics*: "Friendship [*philia*] appears to be the bond of the state." Related to concord and opposed to sedition, it transcends justice.[83]

Speaking in Tongues

Chapter 14 returns to spiritual gifts, notably to the "talking in tongues" already mentioned as the last and least gift (12:28; 13:1). Paul does not attack the practice head on, although he preferred speaking five words with his mind than thousands with a tongue. "Building up the *ecclesia*" is supremely important. Analogies show the importance of rational communication. Musical intruments must sound distinct notes; otherwise, no one will know what is being played. If you are not understood, you will be speaking to the air (14:9).[84] All languages have meaning, but unless I know what the meaning is, "I will be a foreigner to the speaker and the speaker a foreigner to me" (14:11). Paul is concerned with linguistic, not cultural, barbarians, just as in the early Greek texts that deal with the topic. *Iliad* 2.867 speaks of Carians who speak a foreign language (*barbarophônoi*), as birds do in Aristophanes' *Birds* 199.[85] The Roman poet Ovid, an exile in Pontus, speaks similarly of his isolation: "I am a barbarian here, for I am not understood by anyone."[86] Paul is neither a Greek nor a barbarian (Rom. 1:14), but he inevitably shares such Greek cultural attitudes[87] as in Aristotle's *Politics* (1.1.7), with a quotation from Euripides: "It is right for Greeks to rule barbarians."

Outsiders are likely to view the tongue-talkers as crazy, just as they would view the inspired Gnostics of the *Hermetica*.[88] Paul insists that using the mind is worthwhile and that orderly procedure is best: "God is a God not of disorder but of peace"

(14:33).[89] We note that here Paul's criterion is logical truth, the basis on which he can make ironic remarks about "fools" (2 Cor. 11:16–21). "We cannot do anything against the truth, but only for the truth" (13:8).

Women are told to keep quiet presumably because some of them were troubling the peace of the community. "All things should be done decently and in order" (1 Cor. 14:40). Exactly the same rubric served in 92 B.C. for the public mysteries at Andania in the southwestern Peloponnese, where unseemly behavior was punished by flogging.[90] Kümmel calls the conclusion "notably profane" because the inscription from the mysteries orders twenty rod-bearers to attend the rites and take care that "everything be done decently and in good order."[91] "Religious" may really be a better term than "profane," however.

The Resurrection

At first glance, the fifteenth chapter seems remote from political concerns, but since it deals with the final destiny of the Corinthians as of other Christians, it plainly has a climactic place in the letter. Paul speaks of himself as the last witness of Christ's resurrection but immediately apologizes. He is "the least of the apostles, unfit to be called an apostle, because [he] persecuted the church of God" (15:9). His apostolate is a gift of God: "By the grace of God I am what I am, and his grace toward me has not been in vain. On the contrary, I worked harder than any of them—though it was not I, but the grace of God that is with me" (15:10). Once more he refers to order. The general resurrection will take place in orderly fashion (15:23), and when it takes place everything will be subjected to the Son, who himself will finally be subjected to God (cf. 3:23), "so that God may be everything to everyone" (RSV) or, more probably, "so that God may be in complete control" (15:28).[92] For Paul, cosmic order involves rank and obedience.

Mutual Subjection

Finally, the sixteenth chapter depicts mutual subjection of a more mundane kind (16:1–4). It also speaks of Paul's plans and those of his lieutenant Timothy and his colleague Apollos (16:5–12). The practical conclusion of Paul's discussion occurs in verses 15–18. "Now, brothers and sisters, you know that members of the household of Stephanas [cf. 1:10] were the first converts in Achaia, and they have devoted themselves to the service of the saints; I urge you to put yourselves at the service of such people, and of everyone who works and toils with them." The fellow workers and laborers must include those who have just come to Paul from Corinth. "I rejoice at the coming of Stephanas and Fortunatus and Achaicus, because they have made up for your absence. . . . So give recognition to such persons." Recognition means being subject to such leaders of the Corinthian church and realizing that if Paul was called by God's will to be an apostle (1:1; cf. 12:28), Stephanas and his colleagues were called by God's will in their response to Paul.

The picture of the Corinthians that emerges in this kind of reading is not one of otherworldly Gnostics trying to keep the apostle from interfering with their dreams, but of Greek Christians committed to the liberty of which they heard him speak and apparently interpreting it in the light of conventional ideas of democratic organization. There is something strange about the Corinthians, to be sure. They fantasized about themselves and their achievements, as Paul himself did. We must wonder, however, if some of their strangeness is not due to the way in which Paul presents them. He is determined to uphold divine monarchy, mediated through himself as sent by God. There is no room for "grass roots." All, "Jews or Greeks, slaves or free" (12:13), are members of the one body, which does not function in an egalitarian manner. There are higher gifts and lower gifts (12:31).

4

Some Contemporaries

Demetrius the Cynic

Beyond the links with ideas in Aristotle's *Politics*, there are ties in Paul's thought with the ideas of two later philosophers, both of whom taught at Rome but could have visited Corinth toward the end of Nero's reign.[1] The antimonarchist Cynic Demetrius was fairly close to the more radical Corinthians, while Paul himself had links with the thought of the monarchist Stoic Musonius Rufus. If Demetrius had taught at Corinth before Paul's visit rather than later, we could interpret the political-philosophical ideas current among the Christians as perhaps based on his teaching. But at least his teaching shows what some Corinthians, Paul's opponents, could have found comprehensible and attractive.

Demetrius's way of life combined rigorous asceticism, which he interpreted as "possessing everything," and vigorous hostility to the monarchy. He was not the only teacher of the Cynic-Stoic wise man ideal, which had already influenced some Corinthians. His critical attitude toward the emperors from Caligula onward, however, may have influenced those whose attitude Paul rejected in Romans 13 (written from Corinth). Several texts show Demetrius's view of the emperors.

When the young Caligula offered him a gift of 200,000 sesterces, he laughed and refused it, regarding it as a sum not worth boasting about. "If he meant to tempt me," he said, "I could have been tempted by an offer of the whole empire."[2] On some later occasion he said to Nero, "You threaten me with death, nature threatens you."[3] Philostratus relates that he entered "the most magnificent gymnasium in Rome," just completed by Nero, and delivered a speech against people who bathed. He said they enfeebled and polluted themselves, and he showed that baths were a useless expense. Tigellinus, Nero's pretorian prefect, had him banished from Rome.[4]

Philostratus relates another story, probably fictitious, about the exiled philosophers Demetrius and Musonius at the Isthmus of Corinth, "when Nero was outraging Greece over the games." Demetrius tried to console the fettered Musonius, who had been ordered to dig, but Musonius took his spade, dug it into the earth, and looked up to say, "You are distressed, Demetrius, to see me digging through the Isthmus for Greece; but if you saw me playing the harp like Nero, what would you feel then?"[5] Lucian provides a more likely anecdote about Demetrius at Corinth: "When Demetrius the Cynic was at Corinth and saw some uneducated person reading a most beautiful book [it was the *Bacchae* of Euripides, I think, at the place (1114–52) where the messenger reports the fate of Pentheus and the deed of Agave], he snatched it away and tore it up, saying, 'It is better for Pentheus to be torn to pieces by me once rather than by you repeatedly.'"[6]

Opposition to monarchy by Demetrius and others is reported by Dio Cassius and other historians. "Many including Demetrius the Cynic were moved by Stoic principles and took advantage of the name of philosophy to teach publicly many doctrines not appropriate [*ouk epitédeia*] to the times." Again, "Vespasian expelled from Rome all the philosophers except Musonius; he even deported Demetrius and Hostilianus to islands."[7] The philosophers returned Vespasian's hostility. Vespasian most patiently endured the freedom of his friends, the rhetoric of lawyers, and the obstinacy of philosophers. When Demetrius the Cynic, after being sentenced to banishment, met Vespasian on a journey and did not deign either to rise up or to salute him, but even snarled out some abuse, the Roman contented himself with calling him "dog." Alternatively, Vespasian ordered this message to be spoken to him: "You are doing everything to force me to kill you, but I do not slay a barking dog."[8]

In 70, the Roman Senate commended Musonius for attacking the false testimony of Publius Celer against Barea Soranus, but public opinion condemned Demetrius for defending the obviously guilty Publius and revealing "more selfish interest than honorable purpose," or so Tacitus says.[9] The politician-philosopher Seneca, however, had greatly admired his Cynical behavior and teachings: "Our Demetrius is accustomed to say that for him the talk of the ignorant is like the wind made by the belly. What difference does it make whether the sounds come from above or from below?"[10] "I have seen our Demetrius reclining naked on straw: not just a teacher of truth but a witness to it."[11] "I take about with me Demetrius, the best of men, and talk with him, half-naked as he is, and admire him. I have seen that he lacks nothing. . . . Our Demetrius lives not as despising everything but as handing everything over for others to possess."[12] Specifically, "our Demetrius calls a secure life, without any attacks of fortune, a Dead Sea."[13] Just so, "among the many fine sayings of our Demetrius: 'Nothing seems more unfortunate than a man to whom nothing adverse has ever happened.'"[14] Seneca describes him as "heroic, fighting against all the desires of nature, and poorer than other Cynics because while they forbade possessions he forbade even desire for them."[15]

A lengthy passage in Seneca's treatise *On Benefits*, composed in the year 65, praises Demetrius and ostensibly quotes from him.[16]

> Demetrius the Cynic, in my view a great man even compared with the greatest, is accustomed to say (admirably) that it is better to possess a few maxims of philosophy, but with them at our command and in use, than to learn many things that serve no practical purpose. Just as the best wrestler is not the one thoroughly acquainted with all the postures and grips of the art, which he will seldom use against an opponent, but the one who has well and carefully trained in one or two and eagerly waits for the chance to use them. It makes no difference how much he knows if what he knows is enough to win. So in this study many points give pleasure, few give victory. You may not know what principle causes the ebb and flow of the tides; why every seventh year leaves its mark on human life; why the width of a colonnade viewed from a distance does not keep its true proportion but narrows toward the end, and finally the spaces between columns disappear; why twins are conceived separately but born together; whether in coition one act gives birth to two or each is born from a separate act; why those born together have different fates and, though their births were close together, are far apart in the diversity of their experiences. But it will not harm you much to pass over what it is neither possible nor beneficial to know. Truth, wrapped up, lurks in the deep. Nor can we complain that nature is malevolent, for there is nothing hard to discover except what, when discovered, brings no reward other than the fact of discovery. It placed in the open or nearby everything that makes us better and happier. The soul (*animus*) that despises what happens by chance and endures fears and does not greedily covet infinite wealth but has learned to seek riches from itself; that has cast out fear of gods and men and knows that there is not much to be feared from men, nothing from God; that despises everything by which life is tormented though adorned, and is brought to the realization that death is not the

source of any evil but the end of many evils; that has dedicated itself to virtue and thinks that wherever virtue calls is a smooth path; that born as a social animal for the common good it looks on the world as the universal home of all and opens its conscience to the gods and, respecting itself more than all others, lives as if in public—such a soul, removed from storms, stands on solid ground beneath a serene sky and has reached the knowledge of what is useful and necessary. Everything else is for enjoyment in leisure, for when the soul has once found this safe retreat it may also make excursions into things that bring polish, not strength, to its powers.[17]

Apparently it is Seneca himself who goes on to discuss the Cynic-Stoic wise man to whom everything belongs. He returns to Demetrius later to give more specific praise.[18]

Seneca retired to Campania in 62 and was condemned to death in 65; Tacitus describes his philosophically conducted suicide.[19] Similarly, when another of Nero's critics, Thrasea Paetus, was condemned in 66, he spent his last hours with Demetrius, apparently discussing the nature of soul and the separation of spirit from body.[20] Presumably the discussion went along the lines we find in Seneca's treatise on providence:

> I remember hearing Demetrius say, "I have this one complaint against you, O immortal gods, that you did not earlier make your will known to me, for I should have reached the condition earlier in which I now am after being summoned. Do you wish to take children? I fathered them for you. Do you want some part of my body? Take it; I am not offering you a great gift, soon I shall leave all of it. Do you want my life [*spiritus*]? Why not? I shall not delay while you take back what you gave. You will receive whatever you ask of a willing donor. So what is the difficulty? I should have preferred to give, not give up. What need was there to take away? You could have received it, but even now you will not take it away, for nothing is taken from a man unless he withholds."[21]

The Communist Epiphanes

Another aspect of Paul's opponents' thought appears in the fragments of Epiphanes, son of the Gnostic teacher Carpocrates though not a Gnostic himself. In the second century, he laid emphasis on equality and sexual liberation in *On Justice*, in which he defines the justice of God as egalitarian sharing, confirming the claim by analogies that illustrate the divine law. "The heaven, spread out equally from every side, surrounds the whole earth in a circle. Night reveals that all the stars are equal (against 1 Cor. 15:41). God pours forth the cause of the day and the father of light, the sun, from above[22] equally to all on earth who are able to see, and they all see alike, since the sun does not differentiate rich or poor, people or ruler, fools and wise, females, males, free, slaves."[23]

Following Plato's *Republic*, Epiphanes urged that the idea of private property, "Mine and Thine," slipped in through the laws that cause the earth, money, and even marriage no longer to produce fruit for common use.[24] The laws, unable to punish the ignorance of humankind, cut up and nibbled away the sharing set forth in the divine law.[25] (Aristotle devotes the second book of his *Politics* to criticizing this sort of claim.[26])

Since God made all things to be common property, he united the female with males in common[27] and in the same way united all the animals, showing that justice is universal sharing along with equality. But those thus born have denied the sharing that is a corollary of their origin and say, "Let him who has taken one woman keep her." As male animals, all men can share the female.[28]

Sexual desire is both natural and inevitable. God decreed that strong and ardent desire should be implanted in males for the continuance of humanity; it cannot be controlled by law or custom or any other restraint.[29] The saying in the Decalogue, "Thou shalt not desire," must therefore be understood as if the lawgiver was joking, and he added even more comic words, "thy neighbor's property" (Ex. 20:17). He who gave desire as sustaining the process of birth orders it taken away, though he takes it away from no animal! And by the words "thy neighbor's wife" he adds something even more ridiculous because he forces common property to be private.[30]

These notions are based not on Gnostic revelations but on Cynic-Stoic ideas about what is primitive and natural. In regard to "desire," they obviously reverse Paul's view in Romans 7:7: "I would not have known what it is to covet if the law had not said, 'You shall not covet.'" Epiphanes' treatise, highly unusual for a Christian, may constitute part of the background of Paul's Corinthian opponents.

The Gnostic Prodicus and the Corinthians

Paul's opponents at Corinth resemble not only Cynic-Stoics but also the followers of a certain Prodicus, definitely Gnostics according to Clement of Alexandria.[31] These people called themselves Gnostics and laid emphasis on physical unions, not the spiritual ones of Valentinian Gnostics. Some of their basic doctrines seem to be based on exegesis. They claimed to be "by nature" or "by origin" sons of the supreme God, and they used their noble birth (*eugeneia*; cf. 1 Cor. 1:26) with the freedom (*eleutheria*; 1 Cor. 9:1, 19) of "princes" to live as they wished, since for them the "unwritten law" was king. They were not ruled by anyone, for they were "lords of the Sabbath" (Mark 2:28) and above every human race. Presumably because they were lords, they refused to pray.[32] Clement also noted that they used the controversial apocryphal works of Zoroaster. This probably reflects their Gnostic environment. The Nag Hammadi library includes *Zostrianus*, while the Neoplatonist Porphyry says that Christians and others produced apocalypses of Zoroaster and Zostrianus. Another Neoplatonist refuted *Zostrianus*, and Porphyry himself showed that *Zoroaster* was spurious and modern.[33]

Prodicus cannot have accepted hierarchical church government any more than Demetrius accepted monarchy. Indeed,
Tertullian charged that Gnostics generally had no organization
at all: "It is uncertain who is a catechumen, who a believer. . . .
Today one is a bishop, tomorrow another. Today's deacon will
be a lector tomorrow; today's presbyter, tomorrow's lay-
man."[34] The resemblances suggest that a kind of incipient
democratic (or anarchic) Gnosticism, tinged with philosophy
(or else a philosophy tinged with Gnosticism), may have existed
at Corinth in the middle of the first century. Just so, later Gnostics criticized those "outside our number who name themselves
bishop and also deacons, as if they have received their authority from God."[35] At the end of the century this church was still,
or again, tumultuous, and there was still no bishop. Origen,
however, who lived long after Paul, contrasted the quiet church
(*ecclesia*) of God in first-century Corinth with the quarrelsome
civic assembly (*ecclesia*) there, as well as the councilors (*bouleu-
tai*) of both and the rulers (*archontes*) of both.[36] At least in
theory, the time of Paul's church troubles was long past.

Musonius Rufus the Stoic

Though the Corinthian radicals could have found support in
the teaching of the Cynic Demetrius, Paul himself would have
found an ally in his Stoic rival Musonius Rufus, teacher of both
Epictetus and Dio Chrysostom, though not independently
important as a philosopher. Pohlenz emphasizes his upperclass
(equestrian) origins.[37] Like Demetrius, he was well known to
many senators at Rome, especially those who joined a con-
spiracy to overthrow Nero in a time of chaos. The story that
he was forced to dig at the Isthmus of Corinth is almost certainly a legend, though lifelike.

Between 59 and 63, Nero divorced Octavia, and Poppaea,
whom he took from Otho, urged him to murder his mother
Agrippina. Later he murdered Octavia too and ordered the

execution of Rubellius Plautus, the Stoic great-grandson of Tiberius. It was Musonius who urged this man to "await death in preference to an uncertain and anxious life."[38] There was a catastrophic fire at Rome in 64, but two years later the Armenian king Tiridates, accompanied by other rulers, came there to receive his crown from Nero. Perhaps this visit was the occasion of fragment 8 of Musonius "that kings should study philosophy," which begins with the words, "a king from Syria came to him."[39] Nero, touchy about his own writing, exiled the Stoic Cornutus and then went to Greece to compete in games. In 67, Musonius was banished to the waterless island of Gyara in the Cyclades, returning to Rome only after Nero's suicide and the accession of Galba in 68. Conservative Romans had held great hopes for Galba, leader of a revolt against Nero, but he retained power for only nine months and was killed in mid-January 69. Musonius, asked if he still thought the world was really governed by Providence, replied, "When I argued that the world is governed by Providence, did I ever begin with Galba?"[40] Now Otho came to the throne but lasted for only half a year. If Musonius was banished by Vespasian in 71[41] he obviously was not banished with other philosophers in 72, though he was recalled by Titus, presumably in 79.

Later Christians recognized that Musonius was often close to them. Justin Martyr, for example, referred to his sound moral teaching and claimed him as a martyr for the truth taught by the "seed of the Word."[42] Clement of Alexandria used his writings for long passages in his *Tutor*, though without naming him.[43] Origen knew something about him and, in fact, cited a fragment. (He also thought that Musonius's disciple Epictetus was like Paul because even ordinary people admired him.)[44]

There are parallels between Paul and Musonius, though with different emphases. In contrast to the speculative dreams of the Corinthians, Paul insists on the reality of his social situation: "To the present hour we are hungry and thirsty, we are poorly clothed and beaten and homeless, and we grow weary from the work of our own hands" (1 Cor. 4:11–12; cf. 2 Cor. 11:27). His teaching about the endurance of hardships and on athletic training (1 Cor. 9:24–27) is close to what Musonius says about disciplining ourselves to "cold, heat, thirst, hunger, meagre rations, hard beds, avoidance of pleasures, and patience under suffering."[45] The apostle is "homeless," that is, an exile. Musonius, who experienced exile, says that "if I have been deprived of my country, I have not been deprived of my ability to endure exile."[46] And when he speaks of earning his living, he insists on the importance of "hard work with [one's] own hands."[47] Paul emphasizes these points too.

Paul also tells the Corinthians that "to have lawsuits at all with one another is already a defeat for you," and asks, "Why not rather be wronged? Why not rather be defrauded?" (1 Cor. 6:7). Musonius too held that "to scheme how to bite back the biter and to return evil for evil is the act not of a human being but of a wild beast."[48]

Later we shall see points of contact between Paul's discussion of marriage and sex and that of Musonius, notably in regard to conjugal relations (chapter 7). More generally, in Paul's view, married men and women are anxious about worldly affairs (i.e., how to please their spouses [7:33–34]). Ideal marriage, says Musonius, is based on a love that is perfect and completely shared, with "each striving to outdo the other,"[49] while for Paul marriage interferes with devotion to the Lord. He mentions children of Christians as "holy" (7:14) but says nothing about procreation, perhaps irrelevant because of his eschatological calendar (7:29–31). Musonius, on the other hand, views procreation as an essential feature in marriage.

When Paul discusses the hair of men and women (11:15), he claims that nature gave women long hair as a covering (*peribolaios*), while longhaired men were disgraceful. More reasonably, Musonius claims that the male beard—not long hair—was "provided by nature as a covering (*skepē*)."[50]

As Paul develops and expands some of the Corinthian themes in his letter to the Romans, he begins with the universality of sin, manifested especially in sexual immorality. Because of idolatry, God delivered humanity "to degrading passions. Their woman exchanged natural intercourse for unnatural" (Rom. 1:26). Musonius similarly denounces sexual relations between males as "contrary to nature,"[51] but does not mention those of females.

Paul then turns to describe God's forgiveness as effected in Christ and obtained through baptism. He wants to show that God planned the temporary self-exclusion of Jews from the community (Romans 9–11). Finally, he addresses the practical concerns of the church. Practical love, as in 1 Corinthians, is to govern Christian conduct, but beyond that he emphasizes the duty of obedience to the political authorities given power by God. Indeed, Christians owe both obedience and taxes (13:1–7).

Later Christians at Corinth

The Testimony of *1 Clement*

Toward the end of the first century, a leader in the Roman church wrote a long letter, now known as *1 Clement*, to the church at Corinth, advocating order against insubordination in the community. He certainly relied on 1 Corinthians, which he explicitly called "the letter of the blessed apostle Paul."[52] The changes are conspicuous. For Clement and his readers, whom he addresses as "men and brothers," the church is an army, with "generals, prefects, centurions," and "captains of fifty" (37.1, 3). The last title comes not from the Roman army but from the Old Testament,[53] but the basic point is to compare the church to a Roman institution. In the church, "the rich are to provide for the poor and the poor are to give thanks to God" (38.2). In a key passage, the author apparently inserts political ideas into a traditional pattern of eucharistic prayer,[54] though the political ideas may well be traditional too (see chapter 2).

We might hope that Clement would tell us something about the early history of the Corinthian church, but like other early Christian authors, he paints a golden past to contrast with current decline (1.2–2.8). Church members were once impartial, walking by the ordinances of God. They were subordinate to their rulers (in church and state alike) and paid due honor to the presbyters, the older men among them. Women had a pure conscience, loved and obeyed their husbands, and managed their households well.

Unfortunately, when "all renown and opportunity for expansion were given" them, whether as first-century citizens or as church members, out of their prosperity emerged "rivalry and envy, strife and sedition, persecution and anarchy, even war and captivity. Conflict broke out between the ignoble and the honorable, the disreputable and the reputable, the foolish and the wise, and the young against their elders."[55] Later on, Clement states that the Corinthian community has removed a divinely sanctioned bishop from office (chaps. 40–44) and "because of one or two persons the ancient and well-established Corinthian church is in revolt against the elders" (47.6). He urges the chief rebel to accept voluntary exile for the sake of peace (54.1–3). Clement is describing early Corinthian Christianity simply as background for his current purposes.

Dionysius, Bishop of Corinth

Late in the second century, when Soter was bishop of Rome (166–175), Dionysius, bishop of Corinth, wrote letters to him and other bishops. The church historian Eusebius knew a collection of these and described them briefly, with quotations from a few.[56] Eusebius begins with Dionysius's conventional teaching of "orthodoxy" to the Lacedaemonians (a *civitas libera* under the Romans) and commendation of peace and unity. Then Dionysius mentions the Athenians, calling on them for faith and a "polity" in accord with the gospel but rebuking them for virtual apostasy after the martyrdom of their bishop Publius. He praises Quadratus for zealously reuniting them and mentions that Dionysius the Areopagite (Acts 17:34) had been their first bishop. Writing to the Christians of Nicomedia, the capital of Bithynia, he attacks the heresy of Marcion, who originally came from nearby Pontus. When he praises the church of Gortyna in southern Crete (the capital city of Crete), the other Cretan churches, and Philip (of Gortyna) for their attested good deeds (a conventional form of address?), he warns them too against heresy. In addition, he writes to Amastris and the other churches of Pontus, says that Bacchylides and Elpistus had asked him to write, and names their bishop Palmas. Exhorting them on marriage and chastity, he "commands" them to take back those suspected of falling away into misconduct or heresy.

There is also a letter to Pinytos, bishop of Cnossus in northern Crete (whose city, like Corinth, was a Roman colony), urging him "not to lay a heavy compulsory burden of chastity on the brothers but to consider the weakness of the many." Pinytos in turn urged Dionysius to nourish his people with more solid food, not just milk, lest they "be caught unaware by old age while still treated as children" (cf. 1 Cor. 3:1–2; also "like children," 14:20).

Another letter is addressed to Soter of Rome, praising the church's contributions to "many churches" for the (Christian) poor and mine-workers. He notes that a letter from Soter (perhaps sending funds) is sometimes read in the Corinthian church, as is the letter sent through Clement. Dionysius claims that *1 Clement* "bound together the foundations of the Romans and the Corinthians by Peter and Paul, for both taught together in Corinth and both taught in Italy and were martyred at the same time."[57] The picture is obviously based on

Clement's account of "the good apostles" (*1 Clem.* 5.3–7). The Roman Clement thus provides a precedent for Dionysius's own dealings with other churches. After noting that heretics have falsified his own letters, Dionysius finally "imparts the proper spiritual food" to a woman named Chrysophora.

Pierre Nautin has provided the only adequate analysis of this little dossier of Dionysius's letters.[58] The correspondence must have begun after Dionysius wrote to the church at Amastris in Pontus to oppose the rigorism of its bishop, Palmas, and advocate the readmission of penitents after any kind of sin. Palmas then denounced Dionysius to Soter, bishop of Rome, and Soter wrote Dionysius giving him at least partial support. Dionysius claimed that his own words had been misquoted and stressed his own loyalty. The bishops of Gortyna and Cnossus in Crete were engaged in a similar conflict when Dionysius supported Philip of Gortyna against Pinytus of Cnossus and his view of continence as obligatory. In addition, Dionysius tried to end a schism at Lacedaemon (Sparta) and give support to a new bishop in Athens by recalling the past history of the church there.

To Nautin's literary analysis I must add a few notes on the historical situation in Corinth and in Pontus, especially at Amastris. The position of the Corinthian church was much the same as that of Corinth itself,[59] which as the capital city of Achaea ranked above Athens and lay on trade routes to Italy and Asia Minor, to Crete and the Black Sea. Similarly, Gortyna was the capital city of Crete, as Nicomedia was of Bithynia. An inscription from Amastris in Pontus refers to "Tiberius Claudius Lepidus (son of Lepidus), high priest of [Augustus in] Pontus, prominent citizen."[60] Other references show that Lepidus's criticism of religious fakes was influential. Cagnat adduced a text from the satirist Lucian, who described the charlatan Alexander as attacked by the Epicureans there. Alexander claimed that "Pontus was full of atheists and Christians," and he "hated Amastris most of all the cities in Pontus because he knew that the followers of Lepidus and others like them were numerous in the city; and he would never deliver an oracle to an Amastrian."[61] Such was the situation around the time when Dionysius was writing to the Christians of Nicomedia and Amastris.[62] Later on, to be sure, Christian writers would claim that in the third century when Gregory Thaumaturgus became bishop of Neocaesarea in central Pontus only seventeen Christians lived there.[63] In fact, Christianity had a long history in the area. The first Christians to receive the canonical first epistle of Peter are called "the elect sojourners of the dispersion in Pontus." The Roman legate Pliny reported that he interrogated ex-Christians, apparently in Pontus, who claimed they had abandoned their religion as early as A.D. 90.[64] Considering this history, Dionysius had to reply to his critics in Pontus, especially when they asked him to take a more rigorous stand against backsliding. He had to maintain his position as almost the archbishop of Corinth— and of Greek cities to the north and east.

Part II

Religion and Ritual

5

God and the Gods

Now we turn from Corinthian politics and business to the basic religious concerns of Paul and his converts, beginning with worship of God and the gods (chapter 5), passing on to Christian rites such as Baptism and Eucharist and the concomitant experience of prophecy (chapter 6), and tracing later liturgical developments (chapter 7) to note the concurrence of theology and rhetoric in these prayers.

The Gods

Paul contrasted the "many gods and many lords" of Corinth with the one God and the one Lord (1 Cor. 8:5). He thought of such gods primarily as "idols" and viewed them as having no real existence (8:4). This was not, however, his only claim about them. Idols were nothing, but "what pagans sacrifice, they sacrifice to demons and not to God." The gods were really demons, and Christians could not be partners with them, could not drink the cup of the Lord and the cup of demons, nor "partake of the table of the Lord and the table of demons" (10:20–21).[1]

Idols were present throughout the Hellenistic-Roman world, and the late second-century travel writer Pausanias made it clear that Corinth was full of them.[2] In the first book of his description of Greece he begins with Attica, notably with Athens, and then passes through Megara and the Isthmus of Corinth, where he found a modest temple of Poseidon, on to the Corinthian harbors of Lechaeum, with its sanctuary of Poseidon and, toward Cenchreae, a temple of Artemis. In Cenchreae itself were a temple of Aphrodite and sanctuaries of Asclepius and the Egyptian goddess Isis (2.1.3).[3]

Pausanias does not mention the site half a kilometer northwest of the southwest corner of the archaic temple of Apollo, where broken columns in the Venetian wall (built after 1687) still reveal the site discussed by W. D. Dinsmoor, who analyzed the columns as belonging to "the largest temple in the Peleponnesos" and claimed that Pausanias must have missed it.[4] If so, we may wonder what else he missed.

Near the gate of Corinth, Pausanias found the tombs of the Cynic Diogenes and the famous prostitute Lais, then passed on to the precinct of Bellerophon and the temple of Aphrodite Melaenis, "the black" (2.2.4).[5] Upon reaching the city center, the Agora, he mentions statues of the Ephesian Artemis and Dionysus (2.6) as well as a temple of Tyche (Fortune), a shrine of "all the gods," and statues of Poseidon, Apollo of Claros, Aphrodite, Zeus, Kthonios ("of the underworld"), and Hypsistos ("most high"; 2.8). Nearby was a bronze statue of Athena, and above the Agora one could see a temple of Octavia, sister of the deified emperor Augustus,[6] as well as other statues (3.1). Leaving the Agora on the road to Sikyon he sighted a temple of Apollo (3.6).[7] Near the tomb of Medea's children Mermerus and Pheres (whose shades took vengeance on the Corinthians who had stoned them; 3.7)[8] there was a temple of Athena Chalinitis, the "bridler" (4.1).[9] Nearby was the theater, and above it a sanctuary of Zeus (Jupiter) Capitolinus, obviously Roman in origin like the "temple" of Octavia. Near the theater was the gymnasium, by which were temples of Zeus and Asclepius (4.5).

On the way up to the peak of Acrocorinthus, Pausanias encountered more Egyptian religion when he passed two precincts of Isis, one Isis "of the sea,"[10] the other "Egyptian," and two of Sarapis, one of them "in Canopus."[11] After these came altars to Helios and a sanctuary of Ananké (Necessity) and Bias (Force), into which, he says, it was not customary to enter. Farther up were a temple of the Mother of the Gods, a pillar, and a throne; a temple of the Fates, and a temple of Demeter and Koré, with images not exposed to view.[12] Beyond lay a temple of Hera Bunaea supposedly erected by Bunus son of Hermes (4.6).[13] On the summit of Acrocorinthus was the famous old temple of Aphrodite (5.1). If one turned into the mountain road from Acrocorinth, one would pass a sanctuary of Ilithyia, goddess of childbirth (5.4). Not far from the city on the Corinth-Sikyon road there was a burned temple, which Pausanias's guide identified as belonging to Apollo. Others reported that it had been built for Olympian Zeus but then was destroyed by lightning (5.5). The gods whose shrines and temples are at Corinth, Pausanias notes, are primarily Greek along with a few Romans with Greek equivalents. The Egyptians Isis and Sarapis, presumably introduced by traders or sailors, are the only foreign gods represented.

The only trace of theology in Pausanias's account is expressed in the epithets he occasionally notes. For more we must turn to what Apuleius says about the *ploiaphesia*, or boat festival and Isiac initiation at Cenchreae. In his account, we find a discussion of the epithets of Isis, with her equivalents in other religions, and a listing of her wonderful deeds. Such lists are fairly common. Diodorus Siculus provides another example, as do Hellenistic inscriptions and papyri. Since the inscriptions discuss her cosmic functions, they are related to theology as well as religion. The theological treatment is also found in the essays of Plutarch, the mythological manuals of Cornutus and Pseudo-Heraclitus, the orations of Aelius Aristides, and the writings of innumerable Neoplatonists, and coincides with much of what Christians had to say about cosmic theology.[14] The sacred stories of the various cults varied much more.

A different kind of assembly met in the Jewish synagogue at Corinth, which Paul visited but Pausanias never saw.[15] Acts 17:5–15 tells us that Paul already encountered difficulties with the Jewish community at Thessalonica, and at Corinth he first stayed with Jews and argued in the synagogue (where he had converted Crispus, the synagogue ruler) before turning to the Gentiles (18:1–8). Later "the Jews" brought him before the governor's tribunal. When Gallio refused to hear their case, they gave their new ruler, Sosthenes, a beating, and later Paul left the city, perhaps accompanied by Sosthenes, who joined him in writing 1 Corinthians (1:1). Out of all this conflict, we may be sure, arose Paul's animosity toward "the Jews," who not only killed the Lord Jesus and the prophets but actually drove Paul out and displeased God by hindering his mission (1 Thess. 2:15–16).

But Paul's ideas about idolatry came from his Jewish forebears. In Romans he notes that the wicked turned to idolatry and "exchanged the glory of the immortal God for images resembling a mortal human being or birds or four-footed animals or reptiles. . . . [T]hey exchanged the truth about God for a lie and worshiped and served the creature rather than the Creator, who is blessed forever! Amen." God therefore handed them over to various sexual sins (Rom. 1:23–28).[16] The book of Wisdom likewise denounces idolatry and explains that it leads to such practices as ritual murder and to "sexual perversion, disorder in marriages, adultery, and debauchery" (14:23–27). It insists that the Egyptians worshiped the "most hateful" animals and therefore were oppressed by creatures such as vermin and snakes (15:18–16:1, 5).

Paul's ideas therefore presumably arose in Jewish circles. They were far removed from the "soft monotheism" expressed by Maximus of Tyre, who explained that the essence of the transcendent God cannot be apprehended but only recalled through symbols: "Why should I examine or legislate about images? Let every kind be divine, let it simply be. If the art of Phidias incites Greeks to recall the god, and honor paid animals does the same for Egyptians, a river for others and fire for others; I will not resent the disagreement; let them simply know, let them simply love; let them remember."[17] Paul vehemently disagreed.

Maximus tolerated the Egyptian animal worship that offended many Jews. Many Greeks and Romans were critical too, especially after they heard of a Roman emissary who accidentally killed a cat and apparently was murdered by an Egyptian mob in 59 B.C.[18] But Paul's prime example of animal worship comes from Exodus. In the wilderness, some Israelites worshiped the golden calf they had made. Moses ground it to powder, mixed it with water, and made the people drink (Ex. 32:20). Many more were killed in punishment for this and subsequent sins. These events took place as warning examples, Paul says, and were recorded to instruct Christians, on whom the end of the ages has come (1 Cor. 10:5–11).

Given the episode of the golden calf, it is not surprising that Paul goes beyond attacking animal worship to claim that God does not care about animals at all, thus contradicting the Deuteronomic legislation. Even Philo, usually an allegorizer, sensibly notes that Moses' legislation "extends the idea of moderation and gentleness to the sphere of irrational animals."[19] For example, the Deuteronomic code does not allow domestic animals to work on the Sabbath (5:14), and forbids the boiling of a kid in its mother's milk (14:21) as well as inhumane treatment of birds (22:6–7). In addition, it commands that "you shall not plow with an ox and a donkey yoked together" (22:10) and "you shall not muzzle an ox while it is treading out the grain" (25:4).

Both Philo and Josephus took this legislation literally. As for muzzling, Philo claims that "Moses extended the duty of fair treatment even to irrational animals" and cites "the kindly and benevolent regulation about oxen," which showed how humane the law really was,[20] while Josephus too speaks of not muzzling the oxen and adds, obviously referring to them, "It is not just to exclude from the fruit your fellow workers who have labored to produce it."[21]

Paul rejects the literal meaning, finding the Christian missionary in the ox treading out the grain and claiming that the words of scripture could not possibly refer to animals. "Is it for oxen that God is concerned?"[22] No, the words were written on our account, "for whoever plows should plow in hope and whoever threshes should thresh in hope of a share in the crop" (1 Cor. 9:9–10).[23] For Paul, the ox is not even a coworker.[24] Whereas Philo refers to the yoking of ox and donkey as "unlawful mating," contrary to "the decree of nature" or "the law of nature"[25] (Josephus held a similar view[26]), Paul treats the ox and donkey unevenly yoked or "mismatched" as symbols of believers and unbelievers (2 Cor. 6:14). His allegorical exegesis agrees with the moral interpretation in the *Epistle of Aristeas*.[27] Moses, says this document, did not legislate with curious regulations for the sake of mice and weasel,[28] animals that head the list of unclean creatures in Leviticus 11:29–30. With Epicureans and Stoics, Aristeas opposes "animal rights." Epicurus held that the question of just or unjust does not arise with animals that cannot undertake not to harm or be harmed.[29] Philo sometimes wanted to allegorize the text because "the law does not prescribe for irrational creatures but for those with mind and reason."[30] Paul sympathizes, though he does not explain just why God does not care about animals. He does not appeal to Jesus' sayings that a man is much more valuable than a sheep (Matt. 12:12) or than many sparrows (10:31). Presumably his view is related to his hierarchical vision of the creation, in which animals are at the bottom of the heap. First comes God, then Christ, then humankind, with men superior to women— except in Galatians 3:28 (see chapter 7). Below them are animals, with which God is not concerned.

The One God

The one God is clearly the object of Christian devotion, as 1 Thessalonians, written from Corinth, shows: "You turned to God from idols, to serve a living and true God" (1:10), "the God of peace" (5:23), "who calls you into his own kingdom and glory" (2:12). This God is the Creator whose acts are described in Genesis. It is this God who said, " 'Let light shine out of darkness,' who has shone in our hearts to give the light of the knowledge of the glory of God in the face of Jesus Christ" (2 Cor. 4:6).

Paul begins with the biblical account of the deeds of God, found first of all in the Old Testament and then in the Christian gospel. His analysis of causation, to which we shall presently turn, is based on the biblical stories, starting with the creation according to Genesis. He speaks of Adam in 1 Corinthians 15:45–49 and of Eve in 2 Corinthians 11:3. The events of the exodus have become part of the Christian story, for "our ancestors were all under the cloud, and all passed through the sea." All of them ate the manna and drank from the spiritual rock, but God overthrew most of them in the desert because of the golden calf (1 Cor. 10:1–10).[31] Later God guided and blessed Abraham, who had sons by Sarah and Hagar. Four hundred and thirty years later, God gave the law through angels to Moses (Gal. 3:19) and sent the prophets, who were killed (1 Thess. 2:15).

The specifically Christian sacred story included commandments of the Lord (1 Cor. 7:10; 9:14; cf. 7:12, 25) and traditions about what he did, not only "on the night when he was betrayed" (11:23) but under other circumstances as well. If "the rulers of this age" had understood who their victim was, "they would not have crucified the Lord of glory" (2:8). "Christ died for our sins in accordance with the scriptures, . . . was buried, . . . was raised on the third day in accordance with the scriptures," and then appeared to many witnesses (15:3–7).[32]

There was also a known "mystery" about the future resurrection (15:51–52).[33]

The Victory of God's Order

When Christ returns (15:23–53), he will destroy "every ruler and every authority and power," reigning "until he has put all his enemies under his feet" (cf. Ps. 110:1). At that point "the trumpet will sound, and the dead will be raised imperishable, and we [then alive] will be changed," when we put on the imperishable and immortality. All who belong to him will be raised from the dead, since "the last enemy to be destroyed is death" and "God has put all things in subjection."

The "all things" made subject to Christ obviously do not include God himself, the arranger of subjection, who remains supreme. The subordination of Christ to God in the work of creation will continue at the end, though the absolute transcendence of God means that in a doxology, Paul can disregard prepositional niceties. "O, the depth of the riches and wisdom and knowledge of God! How unsearchable are his judgments and how inscrutable his ways! . . . For from [ex] him and through [di'] him and to [eis] him are all things. To him be the glory forever. Amen" (Rom. 11:33, 36). "When all things are subjected to him, then the Son himself will also be subjected to the one who put all things in subjection under him, so that God may be all in all," or "everything to everyone" (panta en pasin; 1 Cor. 15:28).[34]

Paul's preaching about God in the Corinthian letters depicts the universe as constructed hierarchically, with God supreme and nature far beneath him.[35] Philo too connects theology with sociology, holding that the first of the Ten Commandments "summarizes the laws on God's monarchical rule, stating that there is one First Cause of the world and Ruler and King . . . who has expelled from the purest part of all that exists (the heaven), both oligarchy and mob rule, which attack the state when they arise among the worst of men out of disorder and greed."[36]

First Corinthians 8:4–6 goes further, however, and in a less political direction: "We know that 'no idol in the world really exists,' and that 'there is no God but one.' Indeed, even though there may be so-called gods in heaven or on earth—as in fact there are many gods and many lords[37]—yet for us there is one God, the Father, from whom are all things and for whom we exist, and one Lord, Jesus Christ, through whom are all things and through whom we exist." Presumably this is a Christian meditation on the Shema (Deut. 6:4)—"Hear, O Israel: The LORD is our God, the Lord alone"—introduced into Jewish prayer by the early rabbis. The verse was already cited in Mark's tradition of the words of Jesus (12:29), though it does not appear in Matthew and Luke or in Christian writers before the apologists, who laid little emphasis on it.[38] There is, however, one crucial exception: the proclamation of basic monotheism in the first *Mandate* of the Jewish-Christian *Shepherd of Hermas.* "First of all, believe that God is one, who created and completed everything and made everything out of the nonexistent into existence and contains everything, alone not contained."[39] The influential Irenaeus of Lyons refers to this passage with the words, "Well does the writing say" and then quotes *Hermas* exactly.[40]

Paul seems to have found more theological ideas in the Shema. He or his teachers must have been struck by the identification of "our God" with "the Lord alone." Likewise, Philo had held that in the Bible the terms *theos* (God) and *kyrios* (Lord) referred to two different "powers" of the one God's activity. The title of the creative power is God, since he made and ordered everything, while the title of the kingly power is Lord, since it is right for the maker to rule and control what he has brought into existence.[41] Thus, the Shema could be understood as referring to these two powers, and thus Paul could find a reference to "God our Father," who is "the God and Father of our Lord Jesus Christ," as well as to "the Lord Jesus Christ" himself (2 Cor. 1:2–3). In other words, Christian exegetes could find both Father and Son in the Shema, just as—after Philo—they found the Father and his Word in Genesis 1:3.

The basic philosophical structure of Paul's statement about God and Lord comes from the Greek systematic analysis of causes, usually four in number.[42] Each was associated with a preposition: *ek* ("from," material), *dia* ("through," instrumental), *en* ("in," modal), and *pros* ("for/to," final). Thus, human existence, derived "from" and intended "for" the Father, comes "through" the Lord. (In 1 Corinthians 11:3–12, Paul provides a similar analysis of the relation of the first couple; see chapter 8.) The ascription could also be used without such analysis, as in Romans 11:36: "For from him [God] and through him and to him are all things." Without reference to Judaism or Christianity, this kind of expression appears in what Marcus Aurelius says of nature or the universe: "From you are all things, in you are all, to you are all."[43]

Obviously there is a difference. God is not the material cause of existence, and Philo gives a different list: "by which," the cause; "from which," the material; "through which," the tool or instrument; and "for which," the end or object. The first cause of the universe is God; the material is the four elements; the instrument is the Logos of God, through which it was framed (Gen. 1:3: "Let there be light"); and the final cause is "the goodness of the Fashioner."[44]

This is not to suggest that either the Corinthians or the apostle spent all their time studying causation. Their ideas about God were much fuller (should one say more human?) than that. It is simply to suggest that in the rich mixture of Pauline and Corinthian ideas, the analysis of causes played a significant part.

the meal was disorderly: "When you come together, it is not really to eat the Lord's supper. For when the time comes to eat, each of you goes ahead with your own supper, and one goes hungry and another becomes drunk" (11:20–21). Paul orders them to mind their manners and eat their ordinary meals at home (11:33–34).

Prophecy at Corinth

In Paul's view, prophecy too must be orderly: "When you come together, each one has a hymn, a lesson, a revelation, a tongue, or an interpretation" (14:26). It must also be intelligible, unlike glossolalia: "In church I would rather speak five words with my mind, in order to instruct others also, than ten thousand words in a tongue" (14:19). "If all speak in tongues, and outsiders or unbelievers enter, will they not say that you are out of your mind?" (14:23). What does "out of your mind" mean? The first-century medical writer Celsus begins a discussion on insanity by pointing out that "during the paroxysm of a fever patients are delirious and talk nonsense . . . but when the onslaught of the paroxysm is relieved, at once the mind comes back."[7] This is the kind of temporary craziness Paul has in mind, not anything more lasting. Paul concludes this section with the opposite of crazy: "All things should be done decently and in order" (14:40, discussed in chapter 2).

It is not quite clear whether anyone can "prophesy" or not. In 12:28–31, it appears that not all are prophets, and indeed prophets constitute a class lower than apostles, though all Christians are urged to "strive for the greater gifts." Still, contradictions remain. In 11:5–16, a woman must wear a veil on her head when she prophesies or prays in church, while according to 14:34–35 (as later in 1 Tim. 2:11–12) women are to remain silent in churches: "It is shameful for a woman to speak in church."

Other Accounts of Ancient Rites and Prayers

The rest of the New Testament and Pliny's letter to Trajan also speak of these two major rites, maintained throughout Christian history. Though the New Testament evidence is complex and incomplete, the sources outside 1 Corinthians also indicate that the primary rites of early Christian worship were Baptism, the rite of initiation into the communities, and Eucharist, a common meal celebrating Jesus' living presence within the group, commemorating his last supper with his apostles, and expressing the unity of the church. The basic acts and elements in both rites—washing with water, eating bread, and drinking wine—remained constant, though both rites were interpreted with various symbolic meanings. Symbols came together when Jesus asked his disciples if they could drink the cup he was to drink or be baptized with his baptism (Mark 10:38), and prayed that the cup of suffering and death might pass from him (14:36). And the bread could be identified not only with Jesus' body but with the manna of the exodus.

The New Testament

Baptism

According to the book of Acts, the apostle Peter called on converts to "repent, and be baptized every one of you in the name of Jesus Christ" (2:38; cf. 8:16; 10:48; 19:5). This baptism sometimes preceded, sometimes accompanied, and sometimes followed the gift of the Holy Spirit.[8] Matthew 28:19–20, however, gives it a relatively fixed form when describing how the risen Lord orders his followers to "make disciples of all nations [Gentiles], baptizing them in the name of the Father and of the Son and of the Holy Spirit, and teaching them to obey everything that I have commanded you." Only the evangelist John describes Jesus himself as baptizing, at a time when John the Baptist was also baptizing where there was "abundant water."

A dispute over purification (presumably baptism) arose (John 3:22–30). The statement is corrected a little later in a rather clumsy sentence: "When Jesus learned that the Pharisees had heard, 'Jesus is making and baptizing more disciples than John'—although it was not Jesus himself but his disciples who baptized—he left Judea and started back to Galilee" (4:1–3). Clumsy sentences are not necessarily unintelligible, however, or even secondary. The same Gospel also discusses baptism as a new birth "from above" (3:3–8; cf. Titus 3:6): "No one can enter the kingdom of God without being born of water and Spirit." Some scholars have noticed that nothing is said of water in the rest of Jesus' words, but this fact does not prove that "water" was originally absent from John 3:5.

Christian baptism was evidently related to the baptism initiated by John the Baptist, under whose auspices Jesus himself was baptized. The Jewish historian Josephus presents a view of John's baptism quite different from what we find in the Gospels. He holds that this rite of washing first required virtuous conduct—both justice and piety—and was "acceptable to God, not as pardoning certain sins but as a purification of the body when the soul was already purified by justice."[9] Conceivably he intends to separate the Baptist from Christian baptism, for among the evangelists, Mark (1:4) explicitly calls this "a baptism of repentance for the forgiveness of sins," while both Matthew (3:7–10) and Luke (3:7–9) say John proclaimed the impending wrath of God and insisted that sinners, not the virtuous, must be washed. The baptism of Jesus, no sinner, by John thus presents a theological problem, recognized by Matthew (3:14–15), who has John ask Jesus for baptism, as in the *Gospel of the Ebionites*.[10] The apocryphal *Gospel of the Hebrews* includes this scene:

> Behold, the mother of the Lord and his brothers said to him, "John the Baptist baptizes for the remission of sins; let us go and be baptized by him." But he said to them, "What sin have I done that I should go and

be baptized by him? Unless this very word I speak is ignorance."[11]

Most important for all the evangelists was the notion that a divine voice at the baptism acknowledged Jesus as Son of God. For Mark and Luke, the voice spoke to Jesus; for the *Gospel of the Ebionites* and probably for Matthew, it spoke to John. Mark has the Spirit come down from the heavens like a dove and enter into Jesus (upon him: Matthew and Luke; remaining on him: John).

The story of Jesus' baptism thus included elements prominent later in Christian baptism, such as the forgiveness of sins and the recognition of Jesus as Son of God. The letter to Titus sets forth such an extended interpretation: God "saved us, not because of any works of righteousness that we had done, but according to his mercy, through the water of rebirth and renewal by the Holy Spirit. This Spirit he poured out on us richly through Jesus Christ our Savior" (Titus 3:5–6). Another appears in 1 Peter 3:20–22. Baptism corresponds to the saving of eight persons "through water" in the days of Noah. It is not "a removal of dirt from the body, but an appeal to God for a good conscience, through the resurrection of Jesus Christ."

Eucharist

The tradition about the Last Supper in 1 Corinthians also appears in the Gospel of Mark (14:22–25) and the other Synoptic Gospels.[12] Jesus took bread, blessed it, broke it, and gave it to them, and said, "Take; this is my body." And he took a cup, blessed it, and gave it to them, and they all drank from it. And he said to them, "This is my blood of the covenant, which is poured out for many. Truly I tell you, I will never drink drink of the fruit of the vine until that day when I drink it new in the kingdom of God." Paul's additions, "Do this in remembrance of me," presumably come from actual liturgical practice.

Matthew 26:26–29 remains close to Mark, but both Luke and John make changes. There are rather severe textual problems in the Gospel of Luke. As in the *Didache* (see below) the cup precedes the bread and has no more redemptive significance than the bread itself (22:17–19). In addition, the wine-blood is not described as "poured out for many," except in the poorly attested verse 20. Luke's attitude seems to be reflected in a similar change when he ascribes to Jesus the saying, "I am among you as one who serves" (22:27), instead of what Mark gives (10:45): "The Son of Man came not to be served but to serve, and to give his life a ransom for many." Luke rarely mentions the common meal of the earliest churches, though he tells of disciples on the road to Emmaus who recognize the risen Jesus "in the breaking of bread" (24:30–35), while at Jerusalem the disciples keep "the breaking of bread" (Acts 2:42).[13]

John replaces the scene with foot-washing and discourses on service, as in Luke 22:24–30. Indeed, the archetypical Eucharist for John is not the Last Supper but the miraculous feeding of the five thousand (John 6:1–13). Conceivably this miracle story, narrated in two forms by both Mark and Matthew (Luke omits the second account),[14] had already been connected with the Eucharist in earlier tradition, however, for Mark insists that the stories have a hidden meaning (Mark 8:14–21). In any event, John relates the miracle to the manna God provided in the exodus and explains that Jesus is the bread that came down from heaven (John 6:32–51b). The Spirit gives life while the flesh is of no use, and Jesus' words are spirit and life (6:63). In other verses (6:51c–58), he identifies the bread with his "flesh," which Christians must eat in order to have life in themselves and be raised up on the last day. Like the "water" of John 3:5, eating the flesh and drinking the blood of Jesus does not appear anywhere else in this Gospel. Whether or not these verses originally belonged to John, they anticipate the eucharistic doctrine of Ignatius of Antioch.

The Christian Rites as Described by Pliny

While the Eucharist is clearly visible in the Pauline epistles
and the Apostolic Fathers, a more complete account appears
in a letter of Pliny the Younger, Trajan's legate to Bithynia and
Pontus about 110 (*Epistles* 10.96). He investigated societies
that kept meeting even though he had ordered them closed
down, and we still possess his report, as well as the emperor's
reply. It is especially significant for two reasons. First, it
reveals something of what Pliny was looking for as he questioned the witnesses while relying on Roman precedent. Second, it gives some idea of what Christians were doing, or once
had done, when they met together.

The Roman Precedent: Bacchic Rites in Livy

Cicero in his *Laws* cites a decree of the Senate on the Bacchanalia as the prime precedent for dealing with foreign religious
rites, and Pliny seems to have found what to look for in Livy's
vivid account of "secret rites performed by night."[15] In the year
186 B.C., a "lower-class Greek" had brought them to Etruria,
where the initiations gradually spread among men and women
alike, promoted by "wine, feasting, the mingling of males and
females, youth with age."[16] Finally the Roman consul found
out about them, learning that at first only women had taken
part in the rites, but then one of them from Campania admit-
ted men, made the rites nocturnal, and met increased demand
by initiating for five days a month rather than the previous
three days a year. Both consuls investigated villages outside
Rome, where they found and sentenced two classes of witnesses. They imprisoned initiates who had taken the oath but
committed none of the promised acts, but they put to death
those who had gone on to debauchery, murder, false testimony, forged seals, substitution of wills, and other frauds.[17]
The group's slogan was "consider nothing wrong."[18] As
homosexual practices and murder flourished, the group took

in younger initiates, recently those aged twenty or less, who kept ten days of continence and then celebrated at a banquet. There were wailings, the chant of a choir, and the crash of drums and cymbals.[19] There were prayers from a sacred formula (*carmen*), led by a priest, with oaths taken to perform every crime and act of lust. Men would prophesy in a frenzy, and from a grove near the river "matrons dressed as Bacchantes, with disheveled hair and carrying blazing torches, would run down to the Tiber and plunge their torches in the water, bringing them out still burning—because they contained live sulphur mixed with calcium."[20] There were also ritual washings. The religion had all the frenzy needed for gaining converts.

In response to the consuls' denunciations of sex and violence, the Senate decreed that "there were to be no Bacchanalia at Rome or in Italy." Small groups could be tolerated, but not a common fund or master of ceremonies or priest.[21] A bronze tablet from Calabria cites the decree.[22]

The Roman Investigation of Christians

Pliny apparently relied on this "classic" description of the Bacchanalia when he asked questions about similar matters.[23] (Pliny also asked for Trajan's advice, and the emperor told him that Christians had to be punished for meeting against orders, though unlike Bacchants they were not to be sought after.[24]) He questioned witnesses who said they had never been Christians, and also those who had left the Christian group, some recently, some as long as twenty years before. The ex-Christians told him that

> they were accustomed to meet on a fixed day before dawn to say an antiphonal formula to Christ as to a god and to bind themselves by an oath, not to perform any crime but to abstain from theft, robbery, adultery, the violation of oaths, and the refusal to repay a deposit on demand. After this they were

> accustomed to separate and then meet again for a
> meal that was ordinary and harmless.

Two female "deacons" of the cult had confessed what looked like "extravagant superstition" but nothing criminal. What kind of rite was this? The antiphony was not distinctive; it could be baptismal or eucharistic or something else. The oath concerning the way of life, however, is probably baptismal, while the meal must be the *agapé* or the Eucharist or a combination of the two, just as we shall find it in Justin.

Pliny filtered his language through Livy's account of the Bacchanalia to show how different Christian behavior was. The Bacchic priest dictated prayers "from a sacred formula [*carmen*]," but the initiates indulged in debauchery and swore an oath to practice perjury, to use forged seals and wills and evidence, and to commit murders.[25] The Christians of both sexes also met in darkness before sunrise but were not led by a priest when they spoke their antiphonal *carmen* to Christ.[26] (Instead of a priest they were led by women called "deacons.") These pictures show that non-Christians might well think of Christian worship as rather like the Bacchanalia, even though reliable testimony did not support the notion. Christians remained suspect because of their liturgical practices. Pliny's account, however, contains nothing about the prayers except for the *carmen*. The oath was more important.

Christian Rites in the Apostolic Fathers and the *Didache*

For the prayers that gave verbal content to the Christian rites, there is significant evidence from the end of the first century in the *Didache*, or *Teaching of the Apostles*. This earliest Christian manual of prayer, first discovered in 1875, reflects the life of a Jewish-Christian community in Syria or Egypt (probably not Greece or Asia Minor) and offers models for Baptism and Eucharist in chapters 7–10.[27] The Didachist supplies no explanation of the baptismal rite, while his eucharistic prayers do not refer to Jesus' words of institution at the Last Supper but simply give thanks for the meal and its religious significance, staying close to Jewish models as well as to the Gospel of John. I have arranged the basic liturgical materials as "prayers" and "rubrics."

Rubrics on Baptism (*Did.* 7:1–3)

>Concerning baptism, baptize thus:
>having first rehearsed all these things,[28] baptize in the name of the Father and the Son and the Holy Spirit [Matt. 28:19] in running water;
>if you have no running water, then in other;
>if you cannot baptize in cold, then in warm;
>if you have neither,—pour water three times on the head in the name of the Father and the Son and the Holy Spirit.

Rubrics on Fasting (*Did.* 7:4–8:1)

>Before the baptism the baptizer and the one baptized are to fast, with any others who are able. And you shall tell the one baptized to fast for one or two days before.
>Your fasts are not to be with the hypocrites [Matt. 6:16], for they fast Mondays and Thursdays;
>you fast Wednesdays and Fridays.

Rubric on Prayer (*Did.* 7:2)

>Do not pray as the hypocrites do [Matt. 6:5], but as the Lord commanded in his Gospel:
>"Our Father in heaven, hallowed be your name,
>your kingdom come,
>your will be done as in heaven so on earth,
>give us today our daily bread,
>and forgive us our debt as we forgive our debtors,
>and do not lead us into testing
>but deliver us from the evil one: for yours is
>the power and the glory forever" [Matt. 6:9–13].[29]

Rubric on Prayer (*Did.* 7:3)

> Pray thus three times a day.[30]

Eucharistic Thanksgivings and Doxologies (*Did.* 9:1–3)

> And concerning the eucharist, give thanks thus:
> first over the cup:
> We thank you, our Father,
> for the holy vine of your child[31] David,
> which you made known to us through your child Jesus:
> to you be glory forever.
> And over the broken bread:
> We thank you, our Father,
> for the life and knowledge
> which you made known to us through your child Jesus:
> to you be glory forever.

Prayer for the Church and Doxology (*Did.* 9:4)

> As this broken bread was scattered on the mountains,
> but when gathered became one,
> so let your church be gathered from the ends of the earth
> into your kingdom:
> for yours is the glory and the power
> through Jesus Christ forever.

Rubric on Eucharist (*Did.* 9:5–10:1)

> No one is to eat or drink from your eucharist but those
> baptized in the Lord's name; for of this the Lord said,
> "Do not give what is holy to the dogs" [Matt. 7:6].[32]
> After you are filled give thanks thus:

Prayer of Thanksgiving (*Did.* 10:1–4)

> We thank you, holy Father, for your holy name,
> which you tabernacled in our hearts,
> and for the knowledge and faith and immortality
> which you made known to us through your child Jesus:
> to you be glory forever.
> You, almighty Master, created everything
>   for your name's sake,
> and to humanity gave food and drink

for their enjoyment, that they might give thanks
   to you,[33]
but to us you have given spiritual food and drink and
   eternal life through your child.[34]
Above all we thank you because you are powerful:
   to you be glory forever.

Prayer for the Church (*Did.* 10:5)

Remember, Lord, your church,
to deliver it from all evil
and perfect it in your love,
and gather it, made holy, from the four winds
   into your kingdom, which you prepared for it:[35]
for yours is the power and the glory forever.

Versicle and Response (*Did.* 10:6)

Let grace come and this world pass away.[36]
   Hosanna to the God[37] of David.

Rubric on Holiness (*Did.* 10:6)

If anyone is holy, let him come.
If anyone is not, let him repent.

Final Exclamation (*Did.* 10:6)

Marana tha [Our Lord, come]. Amen.[38]

Thanksgiving over the Ointment[39]

But concerning the words with the ointment give
thanks thus:
   We thank you, O Father, for the ointment which
you made known to us through Jesus your child.
   Yours is glory [and power] forever. Amen.

Final Rubric (*Did.* 10:7)

But allow the prophets to give thanks as they wish.[40]

Additional Rubrics for the Meal (*Did.* 14:1–3)

On the Lord's Day of the Lord come together to break
bread and give thanks, first confessing your

> transgressions so that your sacrifice may be pure.
> Anyone who has a quarrel with his neighbor must
> not meet with you before they are reconciled, so that
> your sacrifice may not be defiled. For this is
> what was said by the Lord: "In every place and time
> offer me a pure sacrifice, for I am a great king,"
> says the Lord, "and my name is marvelous among the
> gentiles" [Mal. 1:11, 14].[41]

Confession and reconciliation must thus precede thanksgiving over bread, as in Matthew 5:23–24.

A significant feature of the Didachist's liturgy is its lack of anything corresponding to what Paul tells the Corinthians about the Lord's Supper, though *Didache* 10.3 agrees with what Paul says about spiritual food and drink. Perhaps the most popular and convincing explanation of the divergences has been that by Hans Lietzmann in his *Messe und Herrenmahl* (1926). According to Lietzmann, the *Didache* preserved the more primitive version of the eucharistic tradition, following the Lucan name "the breaking of the bread" and the lack of a Lord's Supper in the Gospel of John. His conclusion is no longer quite so certain, largely because we still do not know just how the earliest Eucharist was developed, and it is hard to be sure of what was *not* contained in various liturgies.

Clement of Rome

First-century evidence for Christian prayers extends to the Roman letter known as *1 Clement*, written soon after the *Didache*. From it we may perhaps recover a traditional pattern by removing the author's insertions that emphasize his political theme.[42] We can see the prayers elaborately developed beyond the simple affirmations of the Gospels and Paul. Clement begins his prayer abruptly, perhaps because something has been lost in the manuscript tradition (*1 Clem.* 59.2–61). He employs the epithet *pais* ("child" or "servant")—a common designation of Christ in early Christian prayers—only in these chapters.

> [We pray to you] through your beloved child Jesus Christ, through whom you called us from darkness to light, from ignorance to knowledge of the glory of your name, to hope in your name as in the source of all creation, opening the eyes of our heart to know you as the only highest among the highest, the holy one always resting in the holy. You humble the pride of the proud, destroy the calculations of the nations, set the humble on high and make the lofty humble; you make rich and make poor, kill and make alive; you are the only benefactor of spirits and God of all flesh. You look into the abyss, observe human actions, help those in danger, save the hopeless, Creator and Overseer of all spirits. You multiply nations on earth and from all of them have chosen those who love you through Jesus Christ your beloved child, through whom you instruct, sanctify, and honor us.
>
> We ask you, Master, to be our helper and aid. Save those of us in tribulation, have mercy on the humble, raise up the fallen, show yourself to those in need, heal the sick, rebuke those in your people who are deceived; feed the hungry, ransom our prisoners, raise up the weak, encourage the faint-hearted. Let all the nations know you, that you are God alone and Jesus Christ is your child and we are your people and the sheep of your pasture. (*1 Clem.* 59.2–4)

Presumably this biblical-ethical language reflects the liturgical tradition.

Providence and Cosmic Concord

The specific thanksgiving or "eucharist" for the divine work of creation begins with a list of divine attributes:

> You manifested the eternal structure of the universe through your works. You, Lord, created the inhabited

> world; you are faithful in all generations, just in judgments, marvelous in strength and majesty, wise in creating and intelligent in establishing what was made, good toward what is seen and gentle to those who trust in you, merciful and compassionate. (60.1)

While Clement (47.1) certainly knew 1 Corinthians, with its tradition about the Last Supper as well as the doctrine that Christ's "blood was given for us" (21.6), he does not relate these materials to his prayers or, indeed, mention the Last Supper, but instead lays emphasis on cosmic concord. Full praise of harmonious creation and providence appears in *1 Clement* 20. Possibly this was a nonpolitical part of Clement's eucharistic prayer, as Rudolf Knopf suggested in his *Handbuch* commentary of 1920.[43] As prayer, the chapter reads thus:

> The heavens move at your direction and peacefully obey you. Day and night complete the course set by you, not interfering with each other. Sun and moon and the chorus of stars travel on their appointed courses after your ordinance, in harmony and with never a deviation. By your will the earth becomes fruitful at the appointed seasons, yielding food in abundance for man and beast, neither dissenting nor altering any of your decrees, which hold together the inscrutable and indescribable judgments of the abyss and the underworld. Since your creative action has firmly fixed the basin of the boundless sea for the gathering together of the waters, they do not overpass the bounds thus set but obey your commands. (For you said, "Thus far shall you come, and your waves shall break within you" [Job 38:11].) The ocean, which men cannot pass,[44] and the worlds beyond it are governed by the same decrees, O Master. The seasons of spring, summer, autumn, and winter give way to one another in peace; the winds from their quarters perform their service without disturbance, each at its proper time; perennial springs, created for enjoyment and health, unfailingly offer their life-giving breasts to men;[45] the smallest animals accomplish their

mating in harmony and peace. All these things, great Creator and Master of the universe, you ordered to exist in peace and harmony, thus lavishing your goodness on all—and most abundantly on us who have taken refuge in your mercy through our Lord Jesus Christ, to whom be glory and majesty forever and ever. Amen.[46]

A briefer, perhaps alternative, story of creation is closer to Genesis and appears in *1 Clement* 33.3:

By his infinitely great might he established the heavens, and by his incomprehensible understanding he set them in order; and he separated earth from the water that surrounds it and made it firm on the sure foundation of his will; by his decree he commanded the animals that move on it to exist, and he prepared the sea and the animals in it and enclosed them by his power.

Both passages contain the praises of divine power and wisdom as exhibited in the work of creation.

Political Emphases

After providence and cosmic concord, Clement turns to the politics of the cosmic order:

Forgive us our lawlessness and injustice, our transgressions and faults. Count not every sin of your servants, both men and women, but cleanse us with the cleansing of your truth and make straight our ways to walk in holiness of heart and do what is good and pleasing before you and before our rulers. Yes, Master, show your face upon us in peace for goodness, that we may be covered by your mighty hand and delivered from all sin by your uplifted arm, and deliver us from those who hate us unjustly. Give harmony and peace to us and all who dwell upon the earth, as you gave it to our fathers when they called

> upon you in holiness with faith and truth, and grant
> that we may be obedient to your almighty and glori-
> ous name. (60.1–4)

He prays for Christian obedience to "our rulers and governors upon earth," the Roman emperor Domitian and his
subordinates:

> Master, you gave them the authority of rule through
> your excellent and inexpressible might, so that we,
> knowing the glory and honor given them by you,
> might be subject to them, in no way resisting your
> will. To them, Lord, give health, peace, concord, and
> stability, so that they may administer without
> reproach the rule given them by you. For you, Mas-
> ter, heavenly king of the ages, gave the sons of men
> glory and honor and authority over things on earth.
> Lord, direct their will in accordance with what is good
> and pleasing before you, that by religiously adminis-
> tering the authority given them by you in peace and
> humility they may obtain your mercy. (60.4–61.2)

Subjection to political authority meant much to the Paul
who wrote Romans (a letter echoed in Clement's) from
Corinth. So also the Paul of 1 Timothy 2:1–2 urges "that sup-
plications, prayers, intercessions, and thanksgivings be made
for everyone, for kings and all who are in high positions, that
we may lead a quiet and peaceable life." Tertullian too insists
that Christians "are ever making intercession for all the
emperors, asking for them long life, secure rule, a safe home,
brave armies, a faithful senate, and honest people, a quiet
world."[47] Religious rites had political importance. In earlier
days, the great revolt of the Jewish nation against the Romans
was signalled in A.D. 66 when sacrifices for the emperor were
omitted from the temple liturgy at Jerusalem.[48] Obviously
Clement's attitude was the reverse of theirs.

Like the Didachist, Clement concludes his prayer with a
doxology: "To you, who alone can do these good things and

more for us, we offer praise through Jesus Christ, the high priest and guardian of our souls, through whom to you be glory and greatness both now and to the generation of generations and to the ages of ages. Amen" (61.3).

Clement was concerned with the Christian ministry because of Corinthian squabbles over it. He insists that the apostles "appointed their first converts to be bishops and deacons of the future believers" and arranged for the succession of others (chaps. 42 and 44). Only the Latin version adds that they "baptized those who were obedient to the will of God" (42.4), for Clement mentions neither Baptism nor Eucharist explicitly.

Ignatius of Antioch

While the *Didache* describes rites, Ignatius of Antioch is concerned with their basic meaning and with the organizational framework he considers indispensable. He is writing as a Christian to Christians, and his letters tell a good deal about the Eucharist, with use of Johannine, not Pauline, terms, especially the word "flesh," though he calls Ephesian Christians "fellow initiates with Paul" and urges them to "strive to meet more often for thanksgiving (*eucharistia*) to God and to glorify him . . . breaking one bread, which is the drug of immortality, the antidote for not dying but living forever in Jesus Christ." And he tells the Romans, "I want the bread of God, which is the flesh of Jesus Christ . . . and for drink I want his blood, which is imperishable love."[49] The elements must be properly identified. The Philadelphians are to "be zealous to use [only] one eucharist, for there is one flesh of our Lord Jesus Christ and one cup for union with his blood," while at Smyrna there are some who "abstain from eucharist and prayer because they do not acknowledge that the eucharist is the flesh of our Lord Jesus Christ which suffered for our sins."[50] So too Paul had spoken of "discerning the body" (1 Cor. 11:29), though the specific emphasis on the flesh of Jesus is Johannine.

The authority of bishops, "appointed throughout the world" maintains Ignatius's regulations: "No one is to do any of the things pertaining to the church apart from the bishop. A valid eucharist is one celebrated by the bishop or by his appointee. It is not lawful to baptize or hold an *agapé* apart from the bishop." The Didachist had already insisted that in place of a ministry of apostles and prophets his readers were to "appoint for [them]selves bishops and deacons" who "also minister to you the ministry of the prophets and teachers."[51]

Thus, for Ignatius, "he who is within the sanctuary is pure, but he who is outside the sanctuary is not pure; that is, whoever does anything apart from the bishop and the presbytery and the deacons is not pure in conscience." Again, "unless one is within the sanctuary he lacks the bread of God"; this means "join in the assembly." So too the Didachist had stated that only the baptized were to "eat or drink of your eucharist."[52]

The passage about the bishop is one of Ignatius's rare references to baptism, though he wants Christians to regard their baptism as weaponry in their military life,[53] and knows two explanations for the baptism of Jesus. Jesus was baptized by John, "so that all righteousness might be fulfilled by him," as in Matthew 3:15, or so that he might purify the water by submitting to the rite.[54] Neither explanation has anything to do with Paul's ideas about baptism. Ignatius evidently thought the Eucharist was more important, or more controversial, than Baptism.

7

Rites in the Second Century

Liturgy in Justin's Apologetic Theology

Around the year 150, Justin described and interpreted the rites of Baptism and Eucharist in Roman liturgy. By this time his community had eliminated the prophecy Paul mentioned and clarified its approach to the liturgy. Since Justin was writing a defense of Christian life, he did not just describe the rites but supplied theological explanations as well as parallels from comparative religion to show that pagans had stolen their own rites from the biblical revelation. While Justin's Eucharist includes some of the features of 1 Corinthians, he simplified it for liturgical emphasis: "Do this"; "this is my body"; "this is my blood." Otherwise, there are few close echoes of Paul, whose name Justin never mentions, and in the *Apology* there is no quotation from the eucharistic thanksgiving. His *Dialogue with Trypho*, however, offers a more complete picture of the rite.

Baptism

Justin's description of Baptism begins with moral requirements and promises that closely recall those of the *Didache*.

He moves from faith to a promise, then on to the actual rite.

> Those who are persuaded and believe that what is taught and said by us is true, and promise that they can live thus, are taught to fast and pray and ask God for the forgiveness of past sins, while we pray and fast with them. Then they are led by us to where there is water and are reborn as we ourselves were reborn: In the name of the Father of all, the Master God, and our Savior Jesus Christ and the Holy Spirit, they undergo washing in the water at that time. (*Apology* 1.61.2–3)

Justin's own Christian theological explanation follows: "For Christ said, 'Unless you are reborn, you will not enter into the kingdom of the heavens' [cf. John 3:3]. It is obvious to all that those once born cannot enter the wombs of those who bore them [John 3:4]." In addition, saving baptism was foretold in Isaiah 1:16–20 (61.4–8).

> And we learned the explanation [*logos*] of this from the apostles. Since we were born at our first birth by necessity in ignorance, out of a moist seed by the mutual intercourse of parents, and in evil customs and evil ways, so that we may not remain children of necessity and ignorance[1] but become children of free choice and knowledge and obtain the forgiveness of past sins, the name of God the Father and Master of All is invoked in the water over the one who chooses to be reborn and repents of his sins. (He who leads the one to be washed to the washing says only this over him. No one has a name to ascribe to the ineffable God; if anyone should venture to say there is one, he exhibits insane madness.) This washing is called "illumination" because the understanding of those who learn these things is illuminated.[2] And the one illuminated is washed in the name of Jesus Christ, crucified under Pontius Pilate, and in the name of the Holy Spirit, which predicted everything about Jesus through the prophets. (61.9–13)

Next Justin explains parallels in other religions as due to the work of demons:

> And when they had heard this washing proclaimed by the prophet [Isaiah], the demons brought it about that those who visited or approached their temples to offer wine and incense should sprinkle themselves, and finally that those who approach should be washed before they came into the temples where they [the demons] are placed. For those who approach the sacred places and those who worship them [the demons] are ordered by the priests to take off their shoes. (62.1–2)[3]

> And from what has been said you can understand that the demons effected the raising up of the image of the so-called Koré [Persephone] at the springs of waters, saying that she was the daughter of Zeus. . . . In imitation of the Spirit of God, said to be 'borne above the water' [Gen. 1:2], they called Koré the daughter of Zeus.[4] And likewise the evil ones said that Athena was the daughter of Zeus, not from intercourse but, since they knew that God was thinking of making the world through the Logos, through Athena as his first thought.[5] We think it is most ridiculous for the image of a thought to bear a female form. (64.4–5)

We may hope that these accounts of pagan rites are more reliable than Justin's report about a statue set up on the Tiberine Island for Simon Magus. He claims that there was a Latin inscription—*SIMONI DEO SANCTO*, "to Simon the holy god,"[6] but since an inscription found on the island is actually dedicated *Semoni Sanco Sancto Deo Fidio*, to the old Sabine deity "Semo Sancus Sanctus Deus Fidius," we must question Justin's observation or judgment or both.[7] (His other remarks about the history of religions do not seem equally suspect.)

Tertullian follows Justin's example when he provides parallels to Baptism from the mysteries of Isis or Mithras and the Apollonian and Pelusian games.[8]

Eucharist

Justin goes on to tell what happens after baptism. It has introduced the new brother or sister to the central rite of eucharist.

> After we have thus washed the one who is convinced
> and has assented, we take him to the place where
> those called brothers are assembled, so that we may
> intently offer common prayers for ourselves and the
> person illuminated and all others everywhere, that we
> who have learned what is true may be found worthy
> of living in good works and keeping the command-
> ments, so that we may be saved with eternal salvation.
> After the prayers we greet one another with a kiss.
> Then bread and a cup of water mixed with wine are
> offered to the ruler of the brothers; and he takes
> them, giving praise and glory to the Father of the uni-
> verse through the name of the Son and the Holy
> Spirit, and sends up thanksgiving for being made
> worthy of these gifts; he prays at length. When he fin-
> ishes the prayers and the thanksgiving, all the people
> present express their assent by saying *Amen*. (*Amen* in
> Hebrew means "So be it.") When the ruler has given
> thanks and the whole people has assented, those we
> call deacons give each of those present a portion of
> the bread and wine and water over which thanks has
> been offered, and they take it to those not present.
> (*Apology* 65)[9]

As before, Justin offers a theological explanation of the rite,
presumably shared with other Christians at Rome and even
elsewhere:

> And this food we call eucharist. No one can share in
> it but the one who believes our teaching is true and
> has been washed for the forgiveness of sins and
> rebirth, and lives as Christ commanded. We do not
> receive these things as ordinary bread or ordinary
> drink, but just as through the word of God our Sav-
> ior Jesus Christ was incarnate and had flesh and blood
> for our salvation, so also we have been taught that the

food from which our flesh and blood are nourished by digestion,[10] when eucharistized through the word of prayer from him, is the flesh and blood of the incarnate Jesus. In the memoirs, called gospels, the apostles told how they were given orders when Jesus took bread, gave thanks, and said, "Do this in my remembrance, this is my body," and likewise taking the cup and giving thanks said, "This is my blood"; and he gave it only to them. (66.1–3)[11]

Once again he supplies a parallel from the history of religions: "The evil demons imitated this and handed it down in the mysteries of Mithras. You either know or can learn that in the rites bread and a cup of water are set before the initiate, along with some invocations" (66.4).[12] Conceivably they could learn from Justin's own source of information, which may have been the treatise *On the Mysteries of Mithras*, compiled by a certain Pallas in the reign of Hadrian.[13]

Description of Sunday Rites

Justin then turns back to the Eucharist to describe what takes place every Sunday:

After this we always remind one another of these things, and those who prosper help all in need, and we are always together. Over everything we receive we bless the Maker of All through his Son Jesus Christ and the Holy Spirit; and on the day called Sun Day there are common meetings of all who dwell in town or country, and the memoirs of the apostles or the writings of the prophets are read as long as there is time. Then when the reader stops, the ruler delivers a speech of admonition and encouragement for the imitation of these good things. Then we all stand and send up prayers and, as we said, when we stop praying bread and wine and water are brought, and the ruler sends up prayers and thanksgivings to the best of his ability, and the people agrees by saying

> Amen, and the distribution and reception of the eucharistized elements takes place for each and is sent to the absent through the deacons. Each of those who prosper and so desire gives of his own choice what he wishes, and what is collected is deposited with the ruler, and he takes care of orphans and widows and those in need because of sickness or some other cause, those in bonds, and strangers sojourning among us. In short, he is the protector of all in need. (*Apology* 67.1–6)

Once again, he provides a theological explanation:

> We all come together on Sun Day because it is the first day, when God changed darkness and matter and made the universe and Jesus Christ our Savior arose from the dead the same day;[14] for they crucified him the day before Saturn Day, and the day after Saturn Day,[15] which is Sun Day, he appeared to his apostles and disciples and taught the things we have offered for your inspection. (67.7)

Justin describes the Eucharist again in his *Dialogue with Trypho*, including theological explanation and referring to

> the bread of the eucharist, which Jesus Christ our Lord delivered to perform in remembrance of the passion which he suffered for men with souls cleansed from all evil, so that we give thanks to God for creating the world for man with everything in it and for having freed us from the wickedness in which we were born and for having completely destroyed the principalities and powers through the one who became passible in accordance with his will.[16]

In this account, we find a reference to thanksgiving for the creation as in the *Didache* and *1 Clement* (though absent from Justin's more apologetic account), as well as the emphasis on redemption that is lacking in the *Didache*. The two aspects of Eucharist did not have to be separated.

The Kiss of Peace

Justin also mentions a liturgical kiss without comment, stating that "at the end of the prayers we greet one another with a kiss."[17] Earlier, both in the Corinthian letters and in letters written from Corinth, Paul speaks of the "holy kiss."[18] This "holy kiss," later called "kiss of peace" or simply "peace,"[19] may also have been called the "kiss of love" in 1 Peter 5:14.[20]

Did it originate in the synagogue? The evidence for such an origin is poor. F. C. Conybeare followed Aucher's tendentious Latin version of the Armenian Philo[21] and tried to find a kiss of concord and another of love in synagogue rites.[22] Windisch and others rejected Conybeare's idea about rites but mistakenly kept his text of Philo.[23] A story in the Old Testament pseudepigraph *Joseph and Asenath* (19.11) says that kisses communicate life, wisdom, and truth,[24] but this too proves nothing about the existence of a Jewish rite.

Whatever its origins, the Christian kiss was inevitably subject to abuses,[25] and pagans often suspected its morality, just as they questioned the eucharistic language about "body" and "blood." The apologist Athenagoras refers to a command not to "kiss twice because it was pleasurable," and insists on caution "about the kiss or, more precisely, the reverential greeting."[26] Clement of Alexandria differentiates a holy and mystical kiss from one that is unholy, impure, and full of poison.[27] The *Apostolic Tradition* of Hippolytus tells how abuses were to be avoided.[28]

Freedom and Fixity in Thanksgiving

We have seen Paul trying to regulate prophets and the *Didache* encouraging prophets but favoring bishops and deacons along with prophets and teachers. Bishop Ignatius claims to have been inspired by the Spirit when he cried out, "Pay attention to the bishop."[29] In the course of the second century, the prophets raised a more acute problem, especially when sectarian groups, particularly Montanists and Gnostics, insisted on the importance of prophecy. The prophetic prayer of the Valentinian Gnostic Mark is especially significant. According to Irenaeus, this teacher worked on the fantasies of rich women in order to gain control of their persons and possessions, and would promise them prophetic power: "Open your mouth and say anything, and you will prophesy."[30] The simplicity of early Christian ecstasy seems to have disappeared.

In spite of fixed or recommended forms, freedom in prayer was maintained in the church. Even in the third century, the *Apostolic Tradition* ascribed to Hippolytus states that

> the bishop is to give thanks as we have said above. It is quite unnecessary for him to pronounce the same words we have spoken, as if he had to say them by heart in giving thanks to God. Each one is to pray in accordance with his ability. If someone is able to pray at length and to say a solemn prayer, this is good; but if someone says a simpler prayer when he prays no one is to prevent him, provided that he says a prayer of a sound orthodoxy.[31]

To pray according to one's ability naturally involved training in rhetoric, public speaking and its uses. Ancient Christians did not always admire primitive simplicity, and artful rhetorical praises of the beauty and utility of baptismal water and oil appear in writings ascribed to two second-century apologist-bishops, Melito of Sardis and Theophilus of Antioch, late in the reign of Marcus Aurelius.[32] (According to Tertullian, most Christians considered Melito a prophet.[33])

A fragment ascribed to Melito's treatise on baptism[34] begins with "praises of water" as used in the smelting process. Water makes gold and silver bright and beautiful, while it makes copper and iron useful.[35] Indeed, the whole earth yields ample crops when washed by rains and rivers, especially with the rise of the Nile that makes Egypt so fertile.[36] Showers even bathe the air, as well as the rainbow, the mother of rains. Perler claims that Melito's background here is basically biblical, but the details and the outline are not. Reservoirs of water (the celestial ocean) are above the starry firmament, and this water falls on the clouds.[37] The "immeasurable ocean"[38] provides a "strange sight"[39] as a baptistery for sun, moon, and stars, in a "mystical baptism" that feeds and brightens them. In conclusion, Melito attacks the Marcionites, who had removed the account of Jesus' baptism from Luke.[40] "If sun with stars and moon is washed in Ocean, why is Christ not washed in Jordan? King of heavens and leader of creation, rising sun who appeared to the dead in Hades and to mortals on earth, he alone shone forth as sun from heaven."[41] It is hard to imagine a Marcionite converted by the argument, but newly baptized Christians may have found it meaningful.

Melito's contemporary Theophilus of Antioch gives praises not to water but to oil and unction, supposedly the source of the name "Christian."[42] "What is anointed is sweet and useful, not to be ridiculed." (That is, it is beautiful as well as useful.) Ships must be calked, towers and houses whitewashed, infants and athletes anointed with oil, art and ornaments greased and polished.[43] "Furthermore the air and everything under heaven is anointed, so to speak, by light and spirit.[44] Do you not want to be anointed with the oil of God? In fact, we are called Christians because we are anointed with the oil of God."[45] Obviously this is encomiastic interpretation, though elsewhere Theophilus turns to biblical language when speaking of "man's future reception of repentance and remission of sins [cf. Luke 24:47; Acts 2:38] through water and a bath of regeneration [Titus 3:5] for all who approach the truth and are reborn [John 3:3] and receive a blessing from God." He must have thought his apologetic language supplemented the biblical terms.[46]

At Carthage, Tertullian knew writings by both of these apologists. He criticized Melito's rhetoric[47] and claims to have avoided giving "praises of water rather than reasons for baptism."[48] He says he could have provided such praises in an encomium, treating the element's power (*vis*), beauty (*gratia*), abilities (*ingenia*), uses (*officia*), and utility (*instrumentum*) for the world. At least implicitly he was thus criticizing the encomium or *laudes aquae* of Melito.[49] His own argument against Marcion is simply that Marcion's Christ did not reject the baptismal elements of water and oil.[50] Tertullian was not wholly comfortable with the "natural theology" in the rhetoric of the older bishops.[51]

Two generations after Justin, the school of Hippolytus at Rome put together the *Apostolic Tradition* around the time when Callistus, not Hippolytus, became bishop.[52] The anaphora in this liturgy is practically sui generis. It "represents the usage of the Greek-speaking church of Rome, and exercised no influence on the later Roman rite, which presents different features."[53] It begins with liturgical formulas that avoid the creation-providence theme found in witnesses both earlier and later.[54] As Lietzmann put it, "The thanksgiving refers exclusively to the salvation realized through the incarnation of Jesus,"[55] thus sharply differentiating the Christian prayer from the ones offered by either Jews or pagans. "Hippolytus" thus returns to Justin and, beyond him, to Paul's language as recorded in 1 Corinthians.

Part III

Paul on Sexuality

8

Christian Conduct

Our final discussion (chapters 8 and 9) concerns the discussions of Paul and the Corinthians with regard to sexual behavior, both in marriage and outside it, and the related ideas about marriage and the family, especially children. We shall also see how these themes were treated in the subsequent century.

Christian Marriage and Virginity

The marriage legislation of Augustus penalized men over sixty who remarried women under fifty because they were unlikely to produce offspring, and Tiberius forbade such unions. To be sure, by the time when Paul was writing to the Corinthians the emperor Claudius was allowing the unions once more.[1] The goals of Christian society, however, came to diverge from those of the emperors. Justin refers to Christian men and women "of sixty or seventy years, disciples of Christ from childhood, who remain incorrupt,"[2] that is, virginal (cf. Rev. 14:4)—whether married or not. This claim agrees with what Galen wrote about the Christians' unusual "contempt of death, obvious to us every day, as well as their restraint in cohabitation. For they include not only men but also women who refrain from cohabiting all through their lives."[3] Whether their abstinence was good for their health or not remained a topic for debate.[4] Paul definitely believed it was good, as Dale Martin's analysis shows.[5]

Most Christians, to be sure, did not disallow marriage, but like many physicians and prominent Stoic teachers, held that it was only for producing offspring.[6] Despite such austere notions, romantic thoughts did occur among Christians as well as pagans. The *Shepherd of Hermas*, for example, begins when its author, an ex-slave, sees his former owner bathing in the Tiber and helps her out of the water. At this point he muses, "How happy I would be if I had a wife with such beauty and charming ways." This, he writes, was his only thought. (He is replying either to his conscience or to questions raised by others.) Later, however, he learns that he has grievously sinned.[7]

Charges and Countercharges

In spite of, or because of, such attitudes, charges of licentious behavior were regularly brought against Christians in the second century. Specifically, they were accused of promiscuously sharing their wives. How did they reply to the charges?

Blame Pagans

Justin speaks of pagans as "those who prostitute their children and wives."[8] Tertullian more pointedly refers to pagans who "not only use the wives of their friends but also most patiently yield their own to their friends," following the examples of Socrates and Cato "to bear children in other families too."[9]

Texts from the Roman republic and empire provide anecdotal evidence that there was something to such a countercharge. A commentary on the old playwright Lucilius quotes a complaisant husband: "'I am not asleep to everyone' is a proverb that seems to have arisen from a certain Cipius, who was called 'Alongside-snorer' because he pretended to be sleeping so that his wife might commit adultery with more impunity."[10] Plutarch generalizes: "A man fond of pleasure makes his wife meretricious and licentious. . . . Many have shared their sexual pleasures, offering not only their girl friends but also their wives." He repeats the story of Cipius, but names a certain Gabba, his wife, and Maecenas: Gabba said, "It's only for Maecenas that I'm asleep."[11]

In spite of these hesitations, Ovid claimed to have found Roman complaisance tiresome. "Unless you begin to watch your girl," he complained, "she will begin to cease being mine. What do I want with a permissive husband, with one who is a pander?"[12] And Juvenal referred to "the husband [who] takes money from his wife's adulterer and has learned to look at the ceiling, also to snore over his cup with watchful nose." He also cited the complaint of an ex-adulterer who claimed to have saved a marriage at the husband's request.[13]

In the late second century, Apuleius criticized one of his opponents thus:

> His house was all a brothel, his whole family was con-taminated; he was infamous, his wife a whore, the sons too; in short, the doors were knocked on day and night as sport for the young, the windows resounded with songs, the dining room was restive with revelers, the bedroom was a thoroughfare for adulterers; nor did any fear to enter unless he was not bringing the fee to the husband. Thus the disgrace to his bed brought income. Once he was skilled with his own body, now he profits generally from his wife's. And with him many (I do not lie) make contracts for the wife's nights. Hence that well known collusion between husband and wife. If they have paid an ample wage to the woman, no one observes them and they

leave when they will; but those who do not make love
profitable are arrested as adulterers at a given signal
and as they come to leave do not go away before writing a promissory note.[14]

The situation is presented as unusual.

A second-century papyrus letter from Serenus to his sister-
wife Isidora reveals other marital problems.[15] Every day and
evening he venerates the goddess Thoeris "who loves you" and
mourns her absence "since we bathed together." Isidora has
sent him "letters that could have moved a stone," and he
replied by messenger "that same hour." She reports that Kolobos "made me a prostitute," while Kolobos reports that "your
wife said that he himself [Serenus] has sold the chain and
placed me in the boat." Serenus replies, "You say these words
so that I will not be believed any more for my embarkation.
See how many times I have sent to you! Whether you are coming or not, let me know." But when we have only one letter we
cannot understand all the circumstances. Who was Kolobos?

Blame Gnostics

Seemingly straightforward though legendary accounts by
Christian authors place the blame for tales of promiscuity
on the Gnostics by depicting spouse-sharing among them.
Clement of Alexandria claims that "Nicolaus had a beautiful
wife and after the Savior's ascension he was reproached by the
apostles because of jealousy. He brought her into their midst
and offered her to anyone who wanted to marry her."[16]
Epiphanius draws a different but equally exotic picture of
Nicolaus, who supposedly said, "Anyone who does not have
intercourse every day cannot share in eternal life." Epiphanius
also believed that the sect called Gnostics held their wives in
common. The husband would withdraw from his wife and tell
her, "Get up, perform Agapé with the brother."[17]

Blame Simple-minded Literalists

Origen refers to the possibility that a non-Gnostic Christian husband might let his wife do whatever she wanted and befriend whomever she desired or else might claim to be holy and chaste and by his own abstinence force her to commit adultery.[18] Supposedly this is based on an exegesis of Matthew 19:9 (cf. 5:32): "Whoever divorces his wife, except for unchastity, and marries another commits adultery."[19] More precisely, it exemplifies what Paul said about abstinence in marriage as leading to temptation by Satan (1 Cor. 7:5). The situation also recalls what Ulpian said in the *Digest*: Roman law is not concerned with married women whose husbands allow delinquency out of negligence or some fault or resignation or excessive credulity.[20]

Christian Cannibalism

Christians were also accused of a peculiar kind of ritual cannibalism involving small children.[21] Minucius Felix records the slander as based on the eucharistic rite: "An infant, concealed in bread to deceive the unwary, is placed before the one who performs the rites. That infant disguised by the bread is killed by the novice summoned to strike seemingly harmless blows, with hidden and unseen wounds. Horrible to relate, they thirstily lick up his blood and eagerly distribute portions of him."[22] Many other apologists refer to the legend.[23]

Cannibalism, says Galen, had been forbidden in the Roman world only in his grandparents' time, that is, toward the end of the first century.[24] (Similarly Tertullian tells how in Africa, child sacrifice had recently been stopped.[25]) Perhaps pagans began to use cannibalism as a club against Christians at that time. Christians replied to the charge by denouncing pagan child abuse (see chapter 9).

Against Contraception and Abortion

Most Christians joined many pagans in denouncing abortion and often contraception. In 1 Corinthians 15:8, Paul refers to himself as "an abortion," whatever he may mean exactly by the term,[26] but passes over the current topics of contraception[27] and abortion,[28] widespread in the Greco-Roman world. Literate pagans were often opposed to these practices. One of the oldest witnesses against abortion is the so-called *Hippocratic Oath*: "I will not give a woman an abortive pessary."[29] The laws of a private cult of Zeus at Philadelphia in the first century B.C. forbade both abortion and contraception.[30] Similarly, the Stoic philosopher Musonius says that the lawgivers forbade women both to apply contraceptives and to abort, and fined those who disobeyed.[31] Plutarch discusses the topic several times. He denounces "licentious women who employ abortive drugs and instruments so that they can enjoy being filled again."[32] Two passages in the *Lives* set forth the views of virtuous husbands as against immoral wives. A law ascribed to the ancient Romulus says that a husband can put away his wife for using contraception or abortion,[33] and the Spartan Lycurgus insisted that both abortion and contraceptive drugs destroy the body and put the mother in danger.[34] Unusually, Soranus accepted contraception[35] but opposed abortion.[36] In addition, the rhetorician Theon shows that the topic was a thesis discussed in the schools. He says that abortion involves such questions as whether the fetus is a human being and whether women are not responsible for what is aborted.[37]

Hellenistic Jewish authors rejected both practices. The philosopher Philo discusses miscarriages and abortions but insists that the embryo remains a part of the mother until it is born.[38] In a fragment, he confuses the issue by speaking of "not aborting the seed of men or women with contraceptives and other devices." [39] Josephus even claims that "the law" orders women not to abort the embryo nor get rid of it.[40]

Though there is no evidence for this in the Mosaic law, Josephus clearly reflects both Jewish and Greek attitudes.

Christian authors likewise denounced both abortion and contraception. According to the *Didache*, "You shall not perform magic, you shall not take [contraceptive] drugs, you shall not murder the child in abortion, you shall not kill it when born." This is also the teaching of *Barnabas*: "You shall not murder the child in abortion, nor again shall you kill it when born." So also we read in the *Apostolic Constitutions*: "you shall not murder your child in abortion, nor shall you kill it when born; for everything that is fully formed and receives a soul from God will be avenged as murdered if it is unjustly destroyed."[41] Two apocryphal apocalypses teach the same,[42] and the apologist Athenagoras explicitly states that abortion is murder.[43] Clement of Alexandria presents similar doctrine, like Justin defining marriage as the desire for offspring and adding that it is not the disordered flow of sperm, illegal and irrational.[44] He denounces women who use abortive drugs and abort their humanity along with the embryo,[45] and he uses the pseudepigraphical *Apocalypse of Peter* to provide graphic detail.[46]

Latin Christian authors, from Tertullian onward, express the same doctrine:

> For us murder is absolutely forbidden; it is not permitted for us to destroy even what is conceived in the womb while the [mother's] blood is still being drawn on for the human being. Prohibiting birth is hastening murder, and it makes no difference whether one takes away the life after birth or destroys it as it is being born. The one to be is also a man; the whole fruit is already in the seed.[47]

Elsewhere Tertullian states, "Do you dissolve with drugs the one conceived? I think we are no more allowed to kill the one to be born than the one born."[48] In his treatise *On the Soul*,[49] he follows Soranus to claim that the embryo is an animal and therefore has a soul, "as aborting physicians admit."[50]

In the second century, the Roman antiquarian Aulus Gellius denounced women "who try by evil devices to cause the abortion of the fetus they have conceived, so that their flat belly may not be wrinkled or made to droop by the weight of the burden and the labor of the birth" and claims that "it is an act worthy of public detestation and general abhorrence to kill a human being in its inception, while it is being fashioned and animated in the hands of the artificer Nature."[51]

Finally, Paulus insists that of those who give a cup of abortion (or seduction) drugs, even if without criminal intent but for providing a bad example, those of lower rank are to be sent to the mines, and those of upper rank are to be sent to an island and fined part of their property. If a man or woman dies of the drink, however, the donor is to be sentenced to death.[52]

9

Marital Problems

The problems 1 Corinthians treats in the greatest detail have to do with sexual relationships, chiefly within marriage but also outside it. The kind of comparison with Aristotle we provided for the life of the community in chapter 3 is not appropriate here, for Aristotle's dissection of marriage does not fit the Corinthian situation, notably when he says that "the relation of husband to wife seems to be aristocratic; he rules because he is fit and rules in masculine affairs, handing over feminine affairs to the wife." Of course the relation is merely oligarchic if he controls everything or if she rules because she is an heiress.[1] These considerations are not especially relevant to Corinth or in Paul's mind, and the utilitarian regulations in the *Politics* are even more remote.[2] Anecdotal evidence for the general Roman situation may be more significant. Such texts illuminate the question of a Corinthian whom Paul denounced for having his father's wife (1 Cor. 5:1).

Some Roman Fathers' Wives

Roman attitudes among the rich and famous in regard to such situations were sometimes ambivalent. Appian tells how the court physician of Seleucus, Erasistratus, discovered that the king's son, Antiochus I, was in love with Stratonice, daughter of Demetrius Poliorcetes and his father's wife. The physician observed that the youth's ailing health improved only in her presence and persuaded the father to cede her to him. Plutarch tells the same story,[3] while the fourth-century emperor Julian says Erasistratus noted the prince's agitated breathing and very rapid heartbeat and traced the symptoms to their cause.[4]

Another case concerns a request first for a married daughter and then for her mother. Plutarch tells the remarkable story that dates from 56 B.C.[5] Quintus Hortensius, who admired the younger Cato, wanted to have children by Cato's daughter Porcia. Since she had already brought forth two sons for her husband Bibulus, he viewed his request as "honorable and good," and appealed to "nature" on the ground that Porcia should not "quench her reproductive power," offering to give her back as soon as she produced for him. When Cato refused the request, since she no longer belonged to him but to Bibulus, Hortensius then asked him for his own pregnant wife, Marcia. Cato was reluctant to decide and left approval up to Marcia's father, consul in 56. The father agreed to give Marcia, presumably now divorced and under his control, to Hortensius but insisted that Cato join him in giving her away. Six years later, when she became a rich widow, Cato married her again.[6] Though his attitude was undoubtedly based on Stoic or Platonic teaching[7] (before committing suicide he was reading Plato's *Phaedo* and the arguments of Hortensius probably come from the *Republic*[8]), it was in tune with the spirit of the times.

The rhetorical *Controversies* by Seneca the Elder describe another republican case, presumably fictitious. The charge is said to be insanity. A man who already had two adolescent sons took a new wife, and when one son became seriously ill the doctors said it was a mental problem. The father went in to his son with drawn sword and asked him to indicate the cause.

After he said he loved the stepmother, his father ceded her to him. Legal and evidential questions then arose. The other son now accused the father of insanity, claiming that his brother should have died rather than be cured immorally. What if he had desired his mother or sister? Some remedies are worse than the dangers. Everything must have been arranged between the stepson and the stepmother. The illness was faked and the father was being ridiculed as in the worst of mimes.[9]

According to the second-century *Institutes* of Gaius, however, Roman law forbade the union of a man with the sister of his father or mother, his mother-in-law or daughter-in-law, his stepdaughter or stepmother.[10] This is what Paul must mean when he claims that not even pagans tolerate such immoral unions, while Corinthian Christians are "puffed up" with pride over the moral situation, like the kings and tyrants Dio Chrysostom says were "puffed up in soul."[11] Why puffed up? W. G. Kümmel points out that no evidence identifies them with "spiritual antinomians,"[12] but parallels do appear among Cynics and early Stoics, and Diogenes' *parrésia* (boldness or freedom of speech or even outrageousness[13]) could be a positive equivalent to Paul's negative "puffed up." Sextus Empiricus cites the permissive views of Persian Magi and Egyptians (criticized, like Canaanites, in Leviticus 18:2), not to mention the Stoics Zeno and Chrysippus, who at least in theory advocated intercourse with one's mother.[14] One would expect that the Corinthians had some ostensible reason to justify their surprising attitude. Did they appeal to philosophy? Paul insists that they should have expelled the offender and, indeed, "delivered such a man to Satan" (5:5). The essential rule for the community (5:2) thus echoes the death sentence of Deuteronomy 17:7: "So you shall purge the evil from your midst" by stoning the offenders. The Old Testament law had long condemned such an act, forbidden in Deuteronomy 22:30 and punishable by death according to Leviticus 20:11. The sinner was also to be ritually cursed, according to

Deuteronomy 27:20. But the Corinthians took pride in themselves instead of stoning the man and the woman. Now the Christian community is to assemble and deliver the man to Satan for the destruction of his body and the salvation of his spirit (5:4–5). Paul says nothing about the woman.

First-Century Emperors

The early Roman emperors made moral pronouncements intended to promote marriage and the raising of children, as well as to maintain class distinctions. In 18 B.C., Augustus provided controversial legislation including the "Julian law on orders of marriage" and the "Julian law on restraining acts of adultery."[15] An ode by the court poet Horace, who the next year supported the legislation in his *Carmen saeculare*, attacks the widespread complacency toward adultery in Augustus's early reign. A wife, he says, "soon seeks younger adulterers among her husband's drinking companions, not choosing a single one to whom she may quickly give illicit joys when the lamps are removed. She openly gets up when summoned (not without her husband's awareness), whether a salesman calls or a master of a Spanish ship, lavish buyer of shameful acts."[16] Suetonius points out that Augustus read in the Senate the speech by Quintus Metellus, censor a century earlier, on increasing the family, to show "that he was not the first to notice such matters."[17] In fact, there were significant changes. Augustus's laws forbade marriages of women who had committed adultery, marriages between free persons of senatorial rank and ex-slaves, and marriages between free men and women with bad reputations. They forbade a husband to kill his adulterous wife or her adulterer but insisted that he divorce her if the evidence was convincing. She was to be banished to an island and lose much of her property. Dio Cassius reports further speeches by Augustus in A.D. 9 praising married men who had children and denouncing the unmarried and childless.[18] This was the year of the Lex Papia Poppaea, from which Claudius later exempted citizens, while Nero reduced informers' rewards by three-quarters.[19]

When Augustus was censor, he failed to face dilemmas created by his own legislation. A young man was accused of taking as a wife a woman already married, with whom he had previously committed adultery. "Augustus was at a loss what to do, not daring to overlook the affair nor yet to administer any rebuke." He simply urged everyone to let bygones be bygones and to concentrate on the future.[20] A singular anecdote related by Seneca tells of a similar dilemma the emperor encountered. A millionaire had placed magnifying mirrors where he could observe his own sexual activities, but his slaves soon killed him. The emperor could not allow the slaves to kill their master, in spite of his immoral behavior. In consequence, Augustus neither prosecuted them nor declared the murder justified. Seneca himself draws the moral lesson that lust uses any means available.[21]

Actors notoriously contributed to the moral problem. Suetonius tells how Augustus tried to deal with one of them. When he "heard that Stephanio, an actor of Roman plays, was waited on by a matron with hair cut short to look like a boy; he had him whipped with rods through the three theatres and then banished him."[22] Enthusiasm for actors was not uncommon in the second century either. Galen tells how he diagnosed a matron who could not sleep but had no fever. When someone mentioned the dancer Pylas her pulse became irregular. Galen suspected her of romantic ideas about Pylas, and to test his theory he had someone mention that Morphus was dancing. Her pulse remained steady and Galen's suspicions were confirmed.[23] Such a story does not "prove" Roman immorality. It surely reflects the reading public's enthusiasm for physicians' diagnostic skill as well as fondness for anecdotes about illicit romance.

Apparently Augustus's successor, Tiberius, was to have his

hands full if he tried to change such attitudes.[24] Indeed, at this time complaints about upperclass women had been increasing. Suetonius comments that "notorious women had begun to profess prostitution and to escape legal penalties by giving up the privileges and rank of matrons." The emperor sent them into exile.[25] Tacitus notes the case of Vistilia, daughter of a praetorian family, who advertised herself for sale on the aediles' list in the year 19. After her husband claimed that he had not invoked the penalty under the Julian law because the sixty days allowed for his deliberation were not yet past, she was banished to the island of Seriphos. In the same year, the Senate decreed that "no woman shall sell her body if her father, grandfather, or husband has been a Roman knight."[26]

Once again from the same year, Josephus relates a romantic story about Egyptian priests at Rome[27] and their attempts to debauch a Roman matron named Paulina. After she refused 200,000 drachmas for intercourse with the Roman equestrian Decius Mundus, his freedwoman offered a quarter of the sum to priests of Isis, one of whom told Paulina that the god Anubis loved her and wanted her to dine and have sex with him. She immediately informed her friends as well as her husband, who assented to her visit since he "trusted her chastity."[28] After supper the temple doors were shut and lamps removed so that Mundus, already concealed within, could spend all night with Paulina. In the morning she told her husband and friends about the divine manifestation of Anubis, but after two days Mundus met her and ridiculed her for credulously saving him his money. She reported the news to her husband, who in turn informed the emperor. Tiberius interrogated the priests and had them crucified, along with the freedwoman, but merely exiled the guilty Mundus because, says Josephus, the crime had been committed "with love" (*meta erôtos*). The temple was razed and the statue of Isis cast into the Tiber.[29] The legal point was that "all persons who lent their aid for the commission of *stuprum* or adultery, or who took money or other valuables as an inducement not to prosecute, rendered themselves liable to the same punishment as the principals," though in this case the principals suffered far less.[30] The unlikely tale attacks the venality of foreign priests and the credulity of a Roman woman, but it may well reflect *la dolce vita* at Rome and elsewhere.

Tacitus, Suetonius, and Josephus date scandals about Egyptian and Jewish rites in the same year, but only Josephus gives details about both groups as involved in hoodwinking Roman matrons. He tells how Fulvia, a woman of high rank, became a proselyte to Judaism and fell under the spell of a crook who was "interpreting the wisdom of the laws of Moses." With three friends he got "purple and gold" from her for the temple in Jerusalem but kept the gift for themselves. Her husband reported to Tiberius, who banished the whole Jewish community from Rome, while the consuls ordered four thousand Jews into military service on Sardinia.[31]

The next attempt at social control used fiscal means. Suetonius speaks of a tax assessed by Caligula (37–41) "from the fees of prostitutes, as much as each earned for one act; to this chapter of the law it was added that those who had ever been prostitutes or panders should be subject to this public tax, and married women were not to be exempt." This may be mere gossip, like the alternative notion that this emperor opened a brothel in the palace in which "matrons and freeborn youths might stand for sale," but it is always hard to be sure.[32]

Stories about the reigns of Claudius (41–54) and Nero (54–68) suggest that the earlier regulations had failed, at least in court circles. The satirist Juvenal, writing half a century later, still recalls, or vividly imagines, the palace prostitution of Claudius's third wife, Messalina. His graphic account of her night life could be more or less correct, though his "information" is half a century old.[33] Is he writing as a satirist? Is he simply hostile toward women?[34] Conceivably he picks Messalina as one example out of many.[35]

In 49, after the death of Messalina, Claudius married his niece Agrippina, who promptly had the philosopher-rhetorician Seneca recalled from exile in Corsica—thus, according to Tacitus, replacing unchastity in the palace by limitless desire for gold.[36] (She shared this lust with Seneca.[37]) Three years later a decree of the Senate forbade women to marry slaves. If a woman did so without the slave's owner's knowledge, she would be ranked as a slave; if with his knowledge, as a freedwoman.[38] Such restrictions on the aristocracy had little to do with Paul or his converts, however.

Like other emperors, Nero made use of moral legislation and claimed that his divorced wife Octavia "had seduced the prefect of the fleet" (who connived with the emperor) and that "conscious of her lusts, she had obtained an abortion." She was banished to the island of Pandateria, then put to death.[39] Tacitus also describes testimony later given against Nero himself:

> Petronius, when condemned to commit suicide, described the crimes of the emperor after the names of the debauched young men and women and the originality of each act, and under his seal sent the document to Nero. As Nero was wondering how the novelties of his nights became known, he recalled Silia, the prominent wife of a senator. Since Nero had admitted her to various lusts and she was very close to Petronius, she was driven into exile because she had not preserved silence about what she had seen and experienced.[40]

Under Domitian, sexual misconduct was even more rigorously punished.[41]

Roman imperial policy thus agreed with Paul's attempts to regulate sex among Christians at Corinth. Though his converts included few if any from the aristocracy, they may well have been influenced by the precedents set at Rome.

Christian Corinth

Several important chapters in 1 Corinthians deal with marital problems because some Corinthian Christians had written Paul a letter about them.[42] He deals first with oral reports about Corinthian life, which we have already discussed, then probably with another oral report (6:12–20). In addition, since the Corinthians' bodies are members of Christ, they cannot make them members of a prostitute, for the man united with a prostitute is one body with her. The Bible says, "The two will be one flesh" (Gen. 2:24). The man united with the Lord, on the other hand, is one spirit with him. Some Corinthians had joined Diogenes the Cynic to argue that sex was as natural as eating,[43] and claimed that just as various foods were for the belly and the belly for foods, so sex is for the body and the body for sex. Paul refused to accept the analogy. God will destroy both the belly and the foods, and the body is not for fornication but for the Lord, while the Lord is for the body, a temple of the Holy Spirit within (6:13–17).

In 6:18, Paul attacks fornication in a new way: "Every [other] sin that a person commits is outside the body; but the fornicator sins against the body itself." Similar ideas appear in the Stoics. Stoics insisted that "the soul is neither helped nor hindered by the body," though Chrysippus held that "everyone who does wrong harms himself undeservedly."[44] Cherniss finds parallels in Musonius, Clement, Epictetus, and Marcus Aurelius.[45] Musonius comes closest to Paul, as Weiss knew.[46] Lietzmann suggests that Paul's generalization is not entirely correct.[47] Since he immediately discusses the body as the temple of the Holy Spirit (6:19), he may have felt this logical weakness himself. He went on to view the body as significant.

In Romans, written from Corinth, he takes another tack, discussing homosexual acts as the consequence of idolatry:

> God gave them up ... to the degrading of their bodies among themselves. .... Their women exchanged[48]

natural intercourse for unnatural, and in the same
way also the men, giving up natural intercourse with
women, were consumed[49] with passion for one
another. Men committed shameless acts[50] with men
and received in their own persons the due penalty of
their error. (1:26–27)

Obviously he is opposed to male homosexual acts (1 Cor. 6:9),
but the modest emphasis given the female in Romans is absent
from the Corinthian letters.[51] Paul shares his use of the term
"contrary to nature" with at least seven Hellenistic authors.[52]

Theological Principles and Practices

We have already seen (chapter 4) that Paul likes to base theological analyses on prepositional distinctions, as when he discusses the relation between God and Christ. Now we see him
speaking similarly about the relation between man and woman
or, more specifically, between husband and wife.

In 1 Corinthians 11:3–12, he states his basic axiom: "I want
you to understand that Christ is the head of every man, and
the husband is the head of his wife, and God is the head of
Christ" (v. 3). A few verses later he draws conclusions: "Man
was not [literally] made from woman, but woman from man.
Neither was man created [literally] for the sake of woman, but
woman for the sake of man" (vv. 8–9). "In the Lord woman is
not independent of man or man independent of woman.[53] For
just as woman came from man,[54] so man comes [literally]
through woman; but all things come from God" (vv. 11–12).[55]
Without such argumentation, Josephus simply states that "the
woman, says the Law [Gen. 3:16], is in all respects inferior to
the man; therefore she is to obey, not to be insulted but to be
governed; for God gave the authority to the husband."[56]

In Galatians 3:28, on the other hand, Paul claims that in
Christ "there is no male and female,"[57] perhaps taking the
expression from Hellenistic Judaism. Philo does say that the

primordial man created by God "after the image" in the first creation narrative was called "male and female" (Gen. 1:26) because "the primary species are in the genus to begin with" though the "man" was (and is) "neither male nor female."[58] The situation of Christians, both male and female, would thus revert to the primeval situation before the creation of the actual human couple. On the other hand, in 1 Corinthians 15:44–49, Paul insists that the first man (Adam) was "psychic," while the last or second man (Christ) was spiritual and from heaven. "Just as we have borne the image of the man of dust, we will also bear the image of the man of heaven." We are not now "heavenly" or "spiritual." H. D. Betz suggests that the differences found in 1 Corinthians "may imply that in [that epistle] Paul has retracted the Galatian position."[59] One should, however, recall the marital mutuality of which Paul speaks (see below).

1 Clement on Women

Though Clement of Rome makes use of 1 Corinthians, in his letter of "counsel" and "petition,"[60] he does not go into any of Paul's subtleties as set forth in the letter but simply states that God "formed man, the most excellent and the greatest of all his creatures in intelligence, in the likeness of his own image by his sacred and blameless hands" (1 Clem. 33.4). His picture of women is not Paul's either. Clement prefers generalizations and presents Jewish tradition about "manly courage" exemplified by Judith, killer of Holofernes, and Esther, victor over Haman (55.3–6). In addition, he praises the Christian women at Rome who were tortured "as Danaids and Dircae" because though weak in body they completed the course of faith (6.2). The daughters of Danaus were given to victors in an athletic contest, while Dirce was bound to the horns of a bull. Presumably this was part of Nero's *spectaculum* in 64.[61]

Corinthian women make trouble, however, and Clement

believes that the Corinthians once taught wives to have "a blameless and pure conscience," to love their husbands "as is suitable," and to manage their households properly (1.3). In more recent times, however, "jealousy has estranged wives from husbands" (a rhetorical generalization; 6.3) and now they stand in need of purity, meekness, gentleness with silence, and sharing their agapé (21.7). Perhaps "silence" comes from Paul.

The Corinthians' Letter

Finally Paul turns to the letter he has received from some of the Corinthians (1 Corinthians 7). They have insisted that "it is well for a man not to touch a woman," but while Paul urges the Corinthians to practice self-control and thus preserve their virginity (1 Cor. 7:1; cf. 7:5, 9), he allows men tempted by desire to marry and insists on the duty of marital intercourse (7:2–9)—though perhaps because of the eschatological timetable, men with wives should "live as though they had none." We have already suggested (p. 34) that the content of Paul's statement (7:29–31) is not essentially eschatological except in the sense that statements of Stoic or Cynic asceticism imply eschatologies. It is also hard to reconcile with what he says about marital duties, equality in marriage, and the reconciliation of separated couples. Indeed, chapter 7 as a whole can be viewed as Paul's attempt to maintain a balance between hierarchy and equality in marriage, between the unmarried, possibly ascetics, and the married, even between male and female. He writes very carefully about his spiritual gifts and those of others (7:6–7) and differentiates what the Lord says from what he himself says (7:10, 12, 25), noting his own "opinion" or "judgment" (7:25, 40). Probably the key to the whole passage appears at the end. The widow who does not remarry, says Paul, "is happier if she remains as she is."[62] And he ascribes this judgment to the Spirit of God (7:39–40).

Paul writes, "The husband should give to his wife her conjugal rights, and likewise the wife to her husband. For the wife does not have authority over her own body, but the husband does; likewise the husband . . ." (7:4–5). Just so, Musonius taught that between husband and wife everything was held in common and nothing was private property, not even their bodies and souls.[63] Such mutuality was emphasized by Hellenistic-Roman Stoics such as Antipater of Tarsus (second century B.C.)[64] and Musonius, by the eclectic Plutarch,[65] and by another Stoic, Hierocles. Both Musonius and the second-century Stoic Hierocles indicated that the married couple "have made everything common property, including their bodies and even their souls."[66] The phrasing, as in the book of Acts, comes from the Pythagoreans. "Everything in common" is theirs, as is the notion of "one body and one soul."[67] Far in the future lies *Tristan und Isolde*. Hellenistic marriage contracts in the papyri reflect a more practical attitude, defining the obligations of each spouse to the other.[68]

Paul ends his discussion with advice not to "deprive" each other, thus keeping his treatment on a legal basis. He agrees with the Mishnah and Solon that the marital "due" should be paid. The Mishnah was practical: The due was to be paid often by the unemployed but not by sailors, while Solon mentioned three times a month for husbands of Athenian heiresses.[69] The basic emphasis is political, for, like Aristotle, Paul knows that for society's sake marriage must be maintained (though the unmarried should count their blessings).

Married couples therefore were not to be divorced, though they could either separate or be reconciled: "To the married I give this command—not I but the Lord—that the wife should not separate from her husband (but if she does separate, let her remain unmarried or else be reconciled to her husband") (7:10–11).

Paul and Justin on Mixed Marriages

Further problems arose in mixed marriages of Christians with pagans (7:12–16): "If any woman has a husband who is an unbeliever, and he consents to live with her, she should not divorce him," for she may be able to "save" him. The same kind of problem is treated in the *Shepherd of Hermas*, which precisely at Rome claimed that neither wife nor husband could continue sexual relations with an unrepentant adulterous spouse, though penitent wives and husbands had to be forgiven. *Hermas* thus disregarded the *Lex Iulia de adulteriis coercendis*.[70]

A century after Paul, Justin shows how the problem could worsen if only one partner turned to Christianity after marriage.

> A woman who lived with a licentious husband had formerly been licentious herself, but when she learned the teachings of Christ she became chaste and tried to persuade her husband to be chaste too. She appealed to the teachings that foretold future punishment in eternal fire for those who did not live chastely and with right reason [*logos orthos*]. When he continued in the same promiscuities he alienated his wife through his actions. The wife now considered sexual intercourse with her husband immoral since he was urging her on to join him contrary to the law of nature [*ho nomos tês physeôs*], and in ways of pleasure contrary to right [*to dikaion*].[71] She wanted to be liberated from the union but forced herself to remain in it when she was rebuked by her own people [Christians], who advised her to remain while she could still hope that her husband might change. But when her husband had gone to Alexandria and was reported as behaving still worse,[72] she gave him what you call the *repudium* and was divorced so that she might not share in his wrongdoing and impiety by remaining in the union either at table or in bed.

Her new behavior contrasted with the old. "That good and noble husband of hers should have been glad she had ended her licentious activities with household servants and hired help, when she enjoyed getting drunk and other wickedness," and wanted him to stop doing the same. But he did not agree, and brought an accusation against the divorced woman, stating that she was a Christian. "She submitted a petition to you the emperor [Antoninus Pius], asking for time to settle her estate and then, after the settlement, to defend herself against the charge, and you permitted this." Her former husband, unable to say anything against her as yet, turned next against her Christian teacher.[73]

She had misbehaved with servants and not, apparently, with slaves. Such unions were forbidden by law. Tacitus says that in the year 52, Claudius "referred to the Senate a motion penalizing women who united with slaves [and] it was resolved that any woman falling to this without the master's knowledge should be considered a slave, but if he had consented she should be considered a freedwoman."[74] A generation later Vespasian "induced the Senate to vote that any woman who joined herself to the slave of another should be considered a bondwoman [*ancilla*]."[75]

In the first century, Josephus related that a Jewish priest had to marry a woman "of his own race [*genos*], without regard to her wealth or other honors." He had to "investigate her pedigree, obtaining the genealogy from the archives."[76] The physician Soranus in the early second century insisted that both class and wealth are irrelevant: "Since people generally marry for children and a family, not for mere pleasant sensations, it is absurd to investigate nobility [*eugeneia*] and abundance of money [*chrématôn periousias*]."[77] Musonius agrees with him: "Those who are marrying must not consider family [*eupatridon*] or money [*chrémata*], if some have acquired fortunes or if they have beautiful bodies; for neither wealth nor beauty nor nobility [*eugeneia*] promotes sharing or harmony, nor are they effective in producing children."[78] No sexual relations with male or female slaves, however, should be permitted.[79]

In the third century when the Christian Hippolytus discussed contraception and abortion, he criticized well-born and
rich Christian women who had begun to use contraceptive
drugs only recently and were wearing tight bindings to abort
what had been conceived. In view of their family and great
wealth, they did not want to have a child by a slave or a worthless man.[80] But Justin did not discuss this aspect of his story.
Naturally Paul had not touched on it, for he insisted that few
Corinthian Christians were either rich or well born.

At first the Roman matron stayed with her husband, thus
following Paul's recommendation in 1 Corinthians 7:10–16.
The husband's view might well be expressed in Plutarch's
Marital Advice: "If some private citizen, incontinent and dissolute in his pleasures, should sin with a prostitute or a servant
girl, his wife must not be indignant or angry, considering that
respect for her makes him share his drunkenness, licentious-
ness and lust with another woman."[81] But Justin's matron had
no reason to think her husband respected her, and she therefore finally followed the counsel of *Hermas*.

She had to settle her estate, which presumably consisted of
the dowry she had brought to the marriage. (This was a stock
theme of Roman comedy.) To administer and settle her estate
took time, both for an accounting and for exchanging accusations with her ex-husband. A similar case appears in Plutarch's
Life of Marius. Fannia separated from her husband and
demanded back her large dowry. The husband accused her of
adultery. Testimony at the trial showed that her husband had
already known she was a dissolute woman when he married her
and lived with her. The judge ruled that he must pay back the
dowry in full while his ex-wife was to be fined a token four cop-
pers because of "infamy."[82] Obviously this could not be the
judgment in regard to Justin's heroine.

She also had to decide whether or not to declare herself a
Christian. The emperor had indeed permitted her to administer her estate and then "to make a defense against the charge

of being a Christian." Her ex-husband was unable to say anything more against her at the moment. She herself does not seem to have been in court with her arrested teacher or to have volunteered any information about her Christianity. Was she still a Christian?

Roman Children

We miss any mention of children in Justin's account, and a Greek physician at Rome was ready to question whether Roman women made good mothers anyway. Soranus suggests that curvature of the spine among Roman infants could be due to cold Tiber water flooding low-lying parts of the city or to too-frequent intercourse of Roman women, especially when drunk. In his opinion, they simply lack experience in raising children and do not have the love (*storgé*) for them that native Greek women do.[83]

Christian Children

In the Gospels, children are mentioned only in the healing of a twelve-year-old girl (Mark 5:41–42) or as models for the kingdom of heaven (Matt. 18:1–4), though Jesus uses them as a metaphor in which the children's bread (except for crumbs) should not be given to dogs (Mark 7:27–28). Like other New Testament writers, Paul rarely mentions children,[84] though he criticizes the imperfection of a child's thinking.[85] Significantly, however, he claims that children derive "holiness" from one Christian parent.[86]

The child's holiness clearly implies the immorality of the widespread "exposure" of newborn infants, though it is not mentioned in the New Testament.[87] A "holy" child obviously cannot be simply left outside to perish. Justin denounces the practice because of its sexual consequences, and as murder.

We have been taught that exposing infants is for
wicked people, principally because we see that practically all of them are brought to fornication, not only
the girls but also the boys, and as the ancients are said
to feed herds of oxen or goats or sheep or horses,[88] so
now children, just for shameful use; and so also a
throng of females and androgynes and fellators
among all peoples exists for this crime. And you take
in wages and taxes and tribute from those you ought
to cut off from your world! And someone who uses
these children for godless, impious and licentious
intercourse may be having sex with his child or relative or brother. And some prostitute their own children and wives, and others are manifestly castrated
for homosexual prostitution and perform the mysteries for the Mother of the Gods.[89]

Though Clement of Rome praises Christians who have
given themselves to bondage in order to ransom others and
adds that "many have delivered themselves to slavery and after
receiving the price have fed others," when Theophilus lists
vices he condemns selling children—in an obviously different
context.[90] Taubenschlag comments on both kinds of selling
thus: "In the Roman sphere, the popular custom of selling
oneself into slavery as well as one's children, though disap-
proved and strongly opposed by imperial law, is still observed
as late as the IV cent. A.D."[91]

Tertullian gives a specific example of the evil of child sales.
He tells of a boy abducted from his parents and later sold in
Rome, where his father accidentally bought him and "used
him in Greek fashion" before sending him in chains to work
in the fields. When an investigation took place, the youth's
parents hanged themselves. The judge Fuscianus assigned
their estate to the boy not as a taxable inheritance but simply
as compensation for the crimes against him.[92] Presumably
Tertullian found this story in a collection of examples to be
used in court cases.[93]

Conclusion

The discussions of sexual conflicts by Paul and other early Christian writers are like what they said about most of the other matters we have dealt with. A Greco-Roman critic would find them dealing only obliquely with the problems of officials, businessmen, traders, shippers, sailors, soldiers, craftsmen, and artists but instead focusing on conflicts in personal and group relations. They build a wall of scripture, philosophy, rhetoric, and theology around the Christian community. To Christian authors, the ordinary business of life, whether at Corinth or elsewhere, was secondary to their cosmic/eschatological worldview. Their thought was at once universal and minutely detailed. The Roman proconsul Gallio regarded the Jewish accusations against Paul as "questions about words and names and your own law" (Acts 18:15), and he would have viewed Paul's discussions in the same light.

Nevertheless, in the course of time the Roman Empire, like Corinth itself, became a ruin, while the Christian church survives. The church's ideas partly replaced and partly assimilated those of the Greco-Roman world. The purpose of this study has been to see how both replacement and assimilation were going on in the early conflicts among Christians.

Notes

Foreword

1. M. Whittaker, *Tatian* Oratio ad Graecos *and Fragments* (Oxford: Clarendon, 1982), 78–81 (fragment from Clement, *Miscellanies* 3.80.3–81.3).
2. See Mitchell, *Heavenly Trumpet.*

Chapter 1. The Journey to Corinth

1. See A. J. Malherbe, *Paul and the Thessalonians* (Philadelphia: Fortress, 1987); L. Fatum, "Brotherhood in Christ," in Moxnes, *Constructing Early Christian Families*, 183–97.
2. Cf. R. M. Grant, *Early Christianity and Society* (San Francisco: Harper & Row, 1977), 66–95.
3. Malherbe, *Paul and the Popular Philosophers*, 35–77.
4. Xenophon, *Memorabilia* 1.1.1; Plato, *Apology* 24b.
5. Jerome, *On Titus* 1:12 (PL 26.607B); cf. Conzelmann, *Apostelgeschichte*, 98.
6. Aratus, *Phenomena* 5. Cf. Aristobulus in Eusebius, *Gospel Preparation* 13.12.6–8; Zeegers-Vander Vorst, *Citations des poètes grecs*, 182n7; van den Hoek, "Aristobulus, Acts, Theophilus," 290–99.
7. Criticizing Jews, he wrote, "Each state has its own religion; ours is for us" (*For Flaccus* 69).
8. The lintel of a Corinthian synagogue is marked [*syna*]*gôgé Eb*[*raiôn*]; *Corinth*, vol. 8, part 1 (1931), no. 111; Wiseman, "Korinth und Rom 1," 547. Second-century Christian-Jewish relations were not close, but there was a certain mutual respect

as expressed by the Jewish interlocutor Trypho, resident in Corinth, in Justin's *Dialogue* (1.3).

9. Polycarp of Smyrna repeats the sexual categories (*Phil.* 5:3), while Theophilus of Antioch adds a few (*Tò Autolycus* 1.2, 14). Old Testament prophets attack idolatry along with adultery (cf. Rom. 1:24–32).

10. At Cenchreae, Paul was acquainted with the "deacon" Phoebe mentioned in Romans 16:1.

Chapter 2. Corinth: City and Church

1. Cited in Frank, *Economic Survey*, 4:475, 483.

2. Cf. Graindor, *Milliardaire antique*, 20–24; see also Ameling, *Herodes Atticus.*

3. Cf. Jesus' parable about hidden treasure (Matt. 13:44).

4. Philostratus, *Lives of the Sophists* 2.1, p. 548; Suetonius, *Vespasian* 13; IG (Corpus Inscriptionum Atticarum) 3.38, 4.

5. Alciphron, *Letters of Parasites* 15, 24.1.

6. Horace (*Odes* 1.7.2) calls Corinth "two-sea'd" (so also Ovid, *Metamorphoses* 5.407; 6.419–20 [Isthmus]; 7.405 [Isthmus]). The Greek equivalent *dithalassos* is not used of our city, though Strabo uses it of the Atlantic Ocean (1.1.8, p. 5) and "so to speak" of the Black Sea (2.5.22, 124). Cf. Corinth "between two seas," Alciphron, *Letters of Parasites* 24.3.

7. W. W. Tarn, *Hellenistic Civilisation*, 3d ed. (London: Arnold, 1952), 251, notes that "most of the wealthiest cities of the world—Seleucia, Antioch, Rhodes, Ephesus, Cyzicus, Delos— were fed by *transit* trade" (italics mine).

8. Strabo 8.6.20, p. 378; see also O. W. Reinmuth, "Isthmien," KP 2 (1967): 1474–75.

9. Thucydides 1.13.5 on the Corinthians: "They had always maintained a market because the Hellenes inside and outside the Peloponnesus, formerly communicating with one another more by land than by sea, had to pass through their territories. . . . And when navigation grew more common among the Hellenes, the Corinthians acquired ships and swept the sea of piracy, providing a market by sea as well as by land and made the city powerful by their cash income."

10. Cicero, *Republic* 2.7–8; Polybius 38.19–22; 39.2. Roman, Cretan, and Carthaginian views of wealth, (6.46.1–3; 56.1–5). Supposedly Carthaginians were poor soldiers because of years of peace (31.21.3); there is a harsh judgment on Alexandria (34.14).

11. Polybius 2.17.10.

12. Ibid. 38.12.5; E. Meyer, "Korinthos," KP 3 (1969), 303.

13. Seneca, *Epistles* 91.10, cited in Frank, *Economic Survey*, 4:467.
14. "Dio Chrysostom," *Oration* 37.36; Aelius Aristides, *Oration* 46(3), 23–31, pp. 369–71 in Keil.
15. See Lenschau, "Korinthos" van der Waele, "Korinthos."
16. Appian, *Punic Wars* 136.
17. See Spawforth, "Roman Corinth."
18. Murphy-O'Connor, *St. Paul's Corinth*, 74 (Propertius, *Elegies* 3.21.19–22), 81 (Philo, *Flaccus* 155), 125 (Philostratus, *Life of Apollonius* 7.10); Ovid, *Tristia* 1.10.9; 11.5–6. Ovid had already called the Isthmus *bimaris* (see note 6).
19. Aelius Aristides, *Oration* 26.13, cited by W. A. Meeks, "Apocalyptic Discourse," *Journal of Religion* 80 (2000): 464.
20. Strabo 8.6.4, p. 369.
21. M. Tolley, "Annexe technical et mechanical" to Raepsaet, "Diolkos de l'Isthme à Corinthe," 260–61.
22. Strabo, *Geography* 8.2.1, 335. On the *diolkos*, see Verdelis, "Diolkos am Isthmus von Corinth"; Verdelis, "Ausgrabungen des Diolkos"; M. S. F. Hood, "Archaeology in Greece, 1956," *Archaeological Reports* 1956, 7: "about 4 m. wide, with two parallel channels 1.50 m. apart, along which travelled the wheels"; Wiseman, *Land of the Ancient Corinthians*, 45–46; MacDonald, "Diolkos"; Raepsaet, "Diolkos de l'Isthme à Corinthe."
23. Pliny, *Natural History* 4.10.
24. This is comparable to the 4 feet 8-1/2 inches of modern railroads. The *diolkos* really had the "ringing grooves" wrongly assigned to railroads by Tennyson in 1842 ("Locksley Hall," line 182).
25. Thucydides 8.7–8. Two years later Aristophanes alluded to the *diolkos* in his *Thesmophoriazusae* 647–48.
26. Polybius 5.101.1–4.
27. See L. R. Taylor and A. B. West, "Latin Elegiacs from Corinth," *AJA* 32 (1928): 9–22; *Corinth* 8.2, 1–4. Lines 3–5 of the inscription read thus: *auspicio [Antoni Marc]i pro consule classis/ Isthmum traductast missaque per pelagus./ Ipse iter profectus Sidam* (Sidé à pirate center, Strabo, *Geography* 14.3.2, p. 664). The name of Marcus Antonius was deleted because he was confused with Caesar's enemy.
28. Cicero, *On the Orator* 1.80.
29. Dio Cassius 51.5.2; Wiseman, "Korinth und Rom 1," 502.
30. G. F. Hertzberg, *Griechische Geschichte seit dem Absterben des antiken Lebens bis zum Gegenwart* 1 (Gotha: Perthes, 1876), 234. Fimmen (RE 9.2259) cites Georgius Phrantzes 1.33 (CSHB 36.96–97; more fully in 1.34, 104) and Theophanes Continuatus 5.61 (CSHB 33.300–301) and notes after Hertzberg that in

the mid-twelfth century it was open for small ships. On the ninth-century situation, see H. Ahrweiler, *Byzance et la mer: la marine de guerre, la politique et les institutions maritimes de Byzance aux viie-xve siècles* (Paris: Presses universitaires, 1966), 102–7, esp. 104.

31. Settlers from Corinth dug a canal through a sandbar on the western island of Leucas (Strabo 1.3.18, p. 59; 10.2.8, p. 452) but by the time of Thucydides, ships were dragged there (3.81.1; 4.8.2). Raepsaet ("Diolkos de l'Isthme à Corinthe," (250) notes that Xerxes dug through the Athos peninsula though the Persians "might very easily have dragged their ships across the isthmus" (Herodotus 7.24).

32. There is a brief notice in Diogenes Laertius 1.99; cf. the list by E. Meyer, "Isthmos," KP 2 (1967): 1475–76.

33. Strabo 1.3.11, p. 54. Engineers told him that water in the Corinthian Gulf, higher than at Cenchreae, would flood the whole area, and Eratosthenes mistakenly agreed with them, as Strabo noted. Darius had similar fears about Egypt.

34. Plutarch, *Caesar* 58.4 (Caesar's initiative); Dio 44.5.1 (Senate's initiative).

35. Philostratus, *Lives of the Sophists* 2.1, pp. 552–53.

36. ILS 8794 or W. Dittenberger, *Sylloge Inscriptionum Graecarum*, 3d ed., 2.814.

37. Suetonius, *Nero* 19.2; Dio 63.16. Pliny (*Natural History* 4.10) lists Demetrius, Caesar, Caligula, and Nero, and calls their work sacrilegious. This work may be the source for Suetonius's very brief notices in *Julius* 44.3 and *Gaius* 21.

38. Philostratus, *Life of Apollonius* 5.19. See van Geytenbeek, *Musonius Rufus and Greek Diatribe*, 5–6.

39. Lucian, *Nero* 1–5 (LCL 8:508–13).

40. Josephus, *Jewish War* 3.540. At the end of the war in 70, however, prisoners were sent to Egypt (6.418), not Greece.

41. See Gerster, "L'Isthme de Corinthe," esp. 229–30; Roux, *Pausanias en Corinthie*, 89 and figures 1–3; Wiseman, *Land of the Ancient Corinthians*, 48–50.

42. Mummius, ILS 20 (*Corinto deleto*). For more information on the temple of Hercules Victor, see Nash, *Pictorial Dictionary of Ancient Rome*, 1:472–74. Livy, *Periochae* 52 (p. 64 in Rossbach) says that Mummius "destroyed Corinth by decree of the Senate because Roman legates had been outraged there" (explained in Strabo, 8.6.23, p. 381).

43. Cicero, *Letters to Friends* 4.5.4 (both Piraeus and Corinth); Cicero, *Republic* 2.7, cited by Feger, "Cicero und die Zerstörung Korinths," 450.

44. See Wiseman, "Korinth und Rom 1," 491–96.
45. Pausanias, 7.16.9.
46. Ibid., 2.1.2.
47. Strabo 8.6.23, p. 381.
48. Appian, *Punic Wars* 136.
49. See Romano, "Post-146 B.C. Land Use in Corinth."
50. Saffrey, "Aphrodite à Corinthe," 362. More detail is provided in Spawforth, "Roman Corinth."
51. Cited in Frank, *Economic Survey* 4:446.
52. Dio 53.12.4; Tacitus, *Annals* 1.76.4 (Dio 58.25.5); Suetonius, *Claudius* 25.3 (Dio 60.24.1).
53. Strabo 8.6.23, p. 382. I agree with M. I. Finley (*The Ancient Economy* [Berkeley, Calif.: University of California Press, 1973], 136): "[Strabo] is unaware of any manufacture for export."
54. Pliny, *Natural History* 34.1, 6–8; Petronius, *Satyricon* 50 (see ch. 52 on Mummius and his looting).
55. Suetonius, *Augustus* 70.2; see Williams, "Roman Corinth as a Commercial Center."
56. Plutarch, *On Borrowing* 831A.
57. Apuleius, *Metamorphoses* 10.18; Julian, *Epistle* 35 (28), 409A.
58. Dio Chrysostom, *Oration* 31.121–22. Cf. Philostratus, *Life of Apollonius of Tyana* 4.22; Mason, "Lucius at Corinth," 162.
59. Pausanias, 2.4.6; Apuleius, *Metamorphoses* 11.8–11, 17.
60. Cf. *Corinth*, vol. 3, part 1.
61. Compare *lesbiazein* (Aristophanes, *Wasps* 1346). Lucian, *On the Nefandous* 28, uses it with *phoinikizein*, as does Galen, *Temperament and Force of Simple Drugs* 10.1 (vol. 12, p. 249 Kühn). Note also the play-title "Corinthiast" mentioned in Athenaeus 7, p. 313c and 13, p. 559a.
62. Quoted, for example, in Strabo 8.6.20, p. 378, and repeated in 12.3.36, p. 559: Comana in Cappadocia is a "little Corinth" with a "multitude of prostitutes" for merchants and soldiers.
63. Plato, *Republic* 3.404D; cf. Aristophanes, *Wealth* 149 (he also plays on *Korinthioi* and *koreis* [bedbugs], in *Clouds* 710–22). Athenaeus collects references to Corinthian prostitutes (13, pp. 573c–574c), especially the famous Lais (pp. 588c–589b).
64. Strabo 8.4.8, p. 361. Conzelmann, "Korinth und die Mädchen," reasonably rejects the whole notion of "sacred prostitutes" at Corinth. Strabo knew oriental Comana better than Corinth.
65. Alciphron, *Letters of Parasites* 24.3.
66. Dio Chrysostom, *Oration* 8.5. Cf. Strabo, 8.6.20, p. 378 (prostitutes and ship captains); Mason, "Lucius of Corinth."
67. Pausanias, 2.2.4; Roux, *Pausanias en Corinthie*, 106: Diogenes Laertius 6.38, 78.

Chapter 3. Religion and Politics

1. Inscriptions related to Paul's letters include one from Delphi that approximately dates Gallio's two-year term as proconsul of Achaea (Acts 18:12). It contains a letter from Tiberius in the twelfth year of his tribunician power when he had been "acclaimed emperor for the 26th time" and refers to his "friend and proconsul L. Junius Gallio." (Murphy-O'Connor, *St. Paul's Corinth*, 141–44, discusses the fragments of text and sets the probable date of the twenty-sixth acclamation in the late spring of A.D. 52.) Inscriptions from Corinth itself mention "the synagogue of the Hebrews" (Acts 18:4; see above), Erastus the aedile (probably not the city treasurer of Rom. 16:23; see *Corinth*, vol. 8, part 3, pp. 99–100); Cadbury, "Erastus of Corinth" and the *macellum* or meat market (1 Cor. 10:25; see *Corinth*, vol. 8, part 2, pp. 100–104; Cadbury, "Macellum of Corinth." There is also the *béma* of the proconsul (Acts 18:12), situated between the central shops in the marketplace (*Corinth*, vol. 1, part 3, 91–109, 128–32).
2. See Malherbe, *Paul and the Popular Philosophers.*
3. Earlier versions of this section were read before the Irish Biblical Association in Dublin, at Kings College, University of London, at Haverford College, at the University of Durham, and as the Richard H. Wilmer Jr. Lecture at the University of Pittsburgh.
4. For the background, see G. E. M. de Ste. Croix, *The Class Struggle in the Ancient World* (Ithaca, N.Y.: Cornell University Press, 1981).
5. J. A. Cramer, *Catenae Graecorum Patrum in Novum Testamentum* (Oxford, 1838–1844, reprinted, Hildesheim: Olms, 1967), 5.214–16 (cf. E. Mühlenberg, "Katenen," *Theologische Real-Encyclopädie* 18 [1989]: 17); for Chrysostom, see PG 61.226D; also 15D, 25A, 153A.
6. See A. A. T. Ehrhardt, *Politische Metaphysik von Solon bis Augustin* 2 (Tübingen: Mohr [Siebeck], 1959); G. Theissen, "Soziale Schichtung in der korinthische Gemeinde," *ZNW* 65 (1974): 232–72.
7. See my essay, "Chains of Being in Early Christianity," in *Christian Beginnings: Apocalypse to History* (London: Variorum, 1983).
8. See H. A. Wolfson, *Philo* (Cambridge, Mass.: Harvard University Press, 1947), 2:375–95.
9. Philo, *Special Laws* 2.231.
10. Clement, *Miscellanies* 7.36.3.
11. Josephus, *Antiquities* 4.223; 6.60–61; 20.251.

12. Josephus, *Against Apion* 2.164–65.
13. Alciphron, *Letters of Parisites* 24.1; Mason, "Lucius at Corinth," 164.
14. See the discussion in Cicero, *Nature of the Gods* 1.10.17 and 67.
15. Aristotle, *Rhetoric* 1.1.12.
16. Cf. Aristotle, *Politics* 5.1.4.
17. Thucydides 4.20.4; cf. 5.31.6.
18. Plutarch, *Moralia* 824C; see also de Ste. Croix, *Class Struggle*, 312.
19. Galen, *On the Use of the Parts of the Body* 14.7 (2.305 Helmreich).
20. Billerbeck, *Kyniker Demetrius*, 11. She also notes the divergence between Lucian/Philostratus and the Roman authors who discuss Demetrius (similarly Aulus Gellius gives an account of Peregrinus quite different from Lucian's). It is not possible to simply pick one or the other.
21. Diogenes Laertius 6.72. Plutarch, *Antony* 24.4, for example, treats "well born" as equivalent to "rich."
22. Aristotle, *Politics* 3.5.7.
23. This is the basis on which Tertullian condemns the polity of the sects (*Prescription of Heretics* 41.8).
24. Aristotle, *Politics* 6.1.6–9.
25. Strabo, *Geography* 14.5.13, 673–74.
26. Diogenes Laertius 7.34.
27. Plutarch, *Cato the Younger* 10, 16.
28. He uses the gentive case to express their relation to God (cf. 3:21–23).
29. Plutarch, *Precepts of Statecraft* 13, 807C.
30. Cicero, *Academica* 2.136 (SVF 3.599); Cicero, *Ends of Good and Evil* 3.75 (SVF 3.591); Philo, *Noah as Planter* 69 (SVF 3.596).
31. Seneca, *Benefits* 7.3.3; 7.4.6; 7.7.1–3.
32. This is what the Cynic Diogenes taught, according to Diogenes Laertius 6.37 (cf. 6.72).
33. Diogenes Laertius 6.24.
34. See SVF 3.597, 588, 600, 603, 617–22. Fragment 603 comes from Philo, *Sobriety* 56 (well-born, rich, glorious, king, free).
35. For survivors carrying placards depicting shipwrecks, see Persius 6.32–33; Juvenal 14.301–2. On the use of placards in court, see Quintilian 6.1.32.
36. Fridrichsen, "Zum Stil der Paulinischen Peristasiskatalogs," *Symbolae Osloenses* 7 (1928), 25–29.
37. Fridrichsen, "Zum Stil der Peristasenkatalogs," Kungliga Humanistika Vetenajeaps-Samfundet Uppsala, Arsbok 1943, 287–89. His references to Charito should be supplemented. They show

the popularity of the motif in Greek rhetoric and at Rome in the first century.

38. Achilles Tatius 5.18.4–5.

39. Aristotle, *Politics* 4.13.1–2.

40. M. Rostovtzeff, *Social and Economic History of the Hellenistic World*, vol. 3 (Oxford: Clarendon, 1941), 613.

41. Robertson, "Corinthian Inscription Recording Honors."

42. Apuleius, *Metamorphoses* 10.33; cf. Mason, "Lucius at Corinth," 163.

43. Weiss (*Erste Korintherbrief* [Göttingen: Vandenhoeck & Ruprecht, 1910], 152, n. 2) cites Plato, *Gorgias* 509C (doing wrong is the greater evil). Cf. Aelius Aristides, *Oration to Plato* 261–75 (LCL 1.422–33); Seneca, *Epistles* 95.52 (Nature teaches that "it is worse to harm than be harmed"); Musonius, fragment 3, p. 40, lines 28–31 Lutz; Epictetus 4.5.10.

44. Cf. Aristotle, *Politics* 6.1.8; 2 Cor. 12:14–19; Polycarp, *Philippians* 11.

45. Ovid, *Fasti* 2.674.

46. Aristotle, *Politics* 7.14.1.

47. Diogenes Laertius 6.29.

48. Hippolytus, *Refutation* 5.8.28.

49. For *telé* at Palmyra, see W. Dittenberger, *Orientis Graeci Inscriptiones Selectae* (Leipzig: Hirzel, 1905), 629; A. Heichelheim in Frank, *Economic Survey* 4.250–54.

50. See list in Newton, *Deity and Diet*, 236.

51. Lietzmann, *An die Korinther,* 49; A. Deissmann, *Light from the Ancient East,* 2d ed. (New York: Doran, 1927), 351 (but *kliné* should not be translated "table"); P Oxy 1.110.

52. He uses arguments from proverbial wisdom, allegorical exegesis, analogy, equity, temple customs, and a saying of Jesus. Compare the analogies for women's veils in chapter 11.

53. Aristotle, *Nicomachean Ethics* 9.6–8.

54. Chadwick, "All Things to All Men," 263.

55. The Isthmian Games offered withered celery (see *Scholia Vetera in Pindari Carmina*, ed. A. B. Drachmann [Leipzig: Teubner, 1903, 1927], 1.112 [on *Olympic Ode* 3.27]; 3.217 [on *Isthmian Ode* 2.19 (e)]; Broneer, "Isthmian Victory Crown," comparing 1 Cor. 9:25).

56. Cf. Dio Chrysostom, *Oration* 8.15: "The noble man regards his hardships as his greatest antagonists and always delights in fighting them night and day, not to win a sprig of parsley as goats do, or for wild olive and pine [awards in various Greek games], but to win happiness and virtue for his whole life." Also 8.18: "Those who know how to box are not hit at all."

57. Aristotle, *Nicomachean Ethics* 8.2.3; cf. 8.10.2; see also Weiss, *Erste Korintherbrief*, 267n4.
58. Aristotle, *Politics* 2.2.6.
59. Marcus Aurelius 5.18.
60. Musonius, fragment 21 (pp. 128–29 in Lutz).
61. Dio Chrysostom, *Encomium on Hair* (LCL 5.332–43).
62. Epictetus 1.16.9–14.
63. Dio Chrysostom, *Oration* 33.48.
64. Aristotle, *Politics* 2.6.5; 5.9.6.
65. Compare his statements on sacrificed meats in 8:13 and 10:25.
66. This means "I do not permit them"—impersonal passive for personal active.
67. These verses may be interpolated; cf. Horrell, *Social Ethos of the Corinthian Correspondence*, 184–95.
68. Plutarch, *Moralia* 142D, 145C.
69. Musonius, fragment 4 (pp. 42–49 in Lutz).
70. Aristotle, *Politics* 7.9.6.
71. Josephus, *Jewish War* 7.323, 410, 418–19.
72. Livy 2.32.9–12.
73. Seneca, *Anger* 2.31.7.
74. W. Nestle, "Der Fabel des Menenius Agrippa," *Klio* 21 (1927): 350–60.
75. For sympathy in this context, see Plato, *Republic* 462C; Sextus Empiricus, *Against Professors* 5.44; Plutarch, *Solon* 18.5.
76. Thucydides 6.18.6.
77. *Interpretation of Knowledge*, pp. 477–80 Robinson.
78. Thus, the noble athlete of Dio Chrysostom, 8.16 (see note on 1 Cor. 9:24–27), contends with hunger, cold, thirst, and gives his body to be whipped, cut, and burned (cf. 1 Cor. 13:3), and is unafraid of hunger, exile, and loss of repute.
79. See Lev. 19:18; Mark 12:31 and parallels; Rom. 3:8; Gal. 5:14; James 2:8. *Didache* 2:7 and *Barnabas* 19:5 are exaggerated: "You shall love some [or 'your neighbor'] more than your life."
80. Aristotle, *Politics* 2.2.6; for a fuller treatment, see *Nicomachean Ethics* 9.8.
81. Augustine, *City of God* 19.14. Other passages treated systematically by A. Nygren, *Agape and Eros* (London: SPCK, 1953), 540.
82. Maximus of Tyre, *Oration* 20.2; cf. E. A. Lehmann and A. Fridrichsen, "1 Kor. 13, eine christliche-stoische Diatribe," *Theologische Studien und Kritiken* (1922): 55–95; Plato, *Symposium* 197D–E.
83. Aristotle, *Nicomachean Ethics* 8.1.4.
84. Cf. "hitting the air" (9:26).
85. See Strabo 14.2.28, 663, with an allusion to Homer.

86. Ovid, *Tristia* 5.10.
87. A Jew could call the hordes of the Syrian kings "barbarous" (2 Macc. 2:21).
88. *Corpus Hermeticum* 9.4.
89. However, in 2 Cor. 12:1–4, Paul insists on his own visions and revelations.
90. W. Dittenberger, *Sylloge Inscriptionum Graecarum*, 3d ed., vol. 2 (Leipzig: Hirzel, 1915–25). Note also that in section XIX (p. 409), there is a "sacred supper" for cult officials.
91. Lietzmann, *An die Korinther*, 121. *Religious* may be a better term than *profane*, however.

Chapter 4. Some Contemporaries

1. This is denied by E. Meyer, "Apollonius von Tyana und die Biographie des Philostratos," *Hermes* 52 (1917): 371–424, esp. 416–17; Billerbeck, *Kyniker Demetrius*, 52.
2. Seneca, *On Benefits* 7.11.1–2.
3. Epictetus 1.25.22.
4. Philostratus, *Life of Apollonius* 4.42 (Nero's "bath," 5.19). For the Thermae Neronianae near the Pantheon, see Nash, *Pictorial Dictionary of Ancient Rome*, 460–64. The baths were finished in 60, while Tigellinus held power in 62 (Billerbeck, *Kyniker Demetrius*, 52); this does not disprove the anecdote.
5. Philostratus, *Life of Apollonius* 5.19; this is rejected by Meyer, "Apollonius von Tyana," 416–17; J. F. Kindstrand, "Demetrius the Cynic," *Philologus* 124 (1980): 83–98, esp. 85.
6. Lucian, *Adversus indoctum* 19. For concern with literary form, see the fragment of "Demetrius" cited by Stobaeus, *Eclogues* 3.8.20, with personified virtues and vices, and the remarks of O. Hense in RE 9.2582–83.
7. Dio Cassius 66.13; 65.13.2.
8. Suetonius, *Vespasian* 13; Dio 65.13.3.
9. Tacitus, *Histories* 4.10; cf. 4.40.
10. Seneca, *Epistles* 91.19.
11. Ibid. 20.9.
12. Ibid. 62.3.
13. Ibid. 67.14; cf. Pausanias, *Description of Greece* 7.5.7: "Living creatures float naturally in it, without swimming."
14. Seneca, *Providence* 3.3; cf. 1 Cor. 4:10–12.
15. Seneca, *Happy Life* 18.3.
16. Seneca, *On Benefits* 7.1.3.
17. The contrast of utility/enjoyment will later emerge as Augustine's use/enjoy.

18. Seneca, *On Benefits* 7.2.5; 7.8.2.
19. Tacitus, *Annals* 15.62–64; cf. Droge and Tabor, *Noble Death*, 17–51.
20. Tacitus, *Annals* 16.34–35. Cf. the discussion in Seneca over whether the soul will be conscious of its departure (*Tranquillity* 14); also the passage from *On Benefits* 7.1.3 cited above.
21. Seneca, *Providence* 5.5–6.
22. James 1:17: "Every generous act of giving, with every perfect gift, is from above, coming down from the Father of lights." God, not the sun, is invariable.
23. Cf. Musonius, fragment 47 (from Epictetus 3.15.14).
24. Plato attacks the notions of Mine and Not Mine in *Republic* 462C (his ideas were Pythagorean, according to Iamblichus, *Pythagorean Life* 167); see Plutarch, *Fraternal Love* 484B. On the connection with marriage, cf. Plutarch, *Marital Precepts* 140D–F; Plutarch, *On Love* 767D–E. Paul uses the word "slip in" of the Mosaic law (Rom. 5:20).
25. Clement, *Miscellanies* 3.7.2–4.
26. Notably Mine and Not Mine in *Politics* 2.1.8.
27. As Clement notes, this comes from Plato (*Republic* 457C). Diogenes the Cynic and the old Stoa concurred (Diogenes Laertius 6.72; 7.33), but Roman Stoics disagreed (e.g., Epictetus 2.4.8–11, also fragment 15).
28. Diogenes held that marriage was simply "the union of him who persuades with her who is persuaded" (Diogenes Laertius 6.72).
29. Clement, *Miscellanies* 3.8.1–2; cf. Musonius, fragment 14 (p. 92, 9–14 lines in Lutz; the Demiurge of mankind implanted mutual desire *not* just in the male); Epictetus 1.6.9.
30. Clement, *Miscellanies* 3.9.1.
31. Ibid. 3.29.3–3.30.1; 7.41.1; 1.69.6.
32. On Prodicus and prayer, see E. Segelberg, "Prayer among the Gnostics?" in *Gnosis and Gnosticism*, ed. M. Krause, Nag Hammadi Studies 8 (Leiden: Brill, 1977), 55.
33. Porphyry, *Life of Plotinus* 16.
34. Tertullian, *Prescription of Heretics* 41.
35. *Apocalypse of Peter* (7:3), p. 376 Robinson.
36. Origen, *Against Celsus* 3.30.
37. M. Pohlenz, *Die Stoa* (Göttingen: Vandenhoek & Ruprecht, 1970), 299; cf. Tacitus, *Histories* 3.81.
38. Tacitus, *Annals* 15.71 (cf. Demetrius and Thrasea Paetus).
39. Visit of a Syrian King, Dio Cassius 63.1.
40. Musonius, fragment 47 from Epictetus 3.15.14.
41. Dio 66.13.

42. Justin, *Apology* 2.8.1. He may well have regarded Musonius's teaching on the purpose of marriage (fragment 13A) as Christian (*Apology* 1.29.1).

43. Clement, *Tutor* 2–3; cf. Wendland, *Quaestiones Musonianae*, esp. pp. 36–37 with Clement's references *en tôi gamikôi logôi* and *en tôi peri enkrateias*.

44. Origen, *Against Celsus* 3.66; Cadiou, *Commentaires inédits des Psaumes*, 118; cf. G. D. Kilpatrick, "A Fragment of Musonius," *Classical Review* 63 (1949): 94. For a contemporary papyrus, see J. E. Powell, *The Rendel Harris Papyri* (Cambridge, Mass.: Cambridge University Press, 1936), 1–5; and J. E. Powell, "Musonius Rufus: *ei panta ta ginomena tekna threpteon*," *Archiv für Papyrusforschung* 12 (1937): 175–78. For more on Musonius's resemblance to Paul, see Origen, *Against Celsus* 6.2.

45. Musonius, fragment 6 (p. 54, lines 12–14 Lutz); cf. fragment 7. Paul's remarks about the games fit the Isthmian Games of his time, but the Cynic-Stoic diatribe, as in Musonius, regularly employed the games as metaphors for life (Weiss, *Este Korintherbrief*, 247–49).

46. Musonius, fragment 9 (p. 74, lines 18–19).

47. Ibid., fragment 11 (pp. 80, line 15; 82, line 24).

48. Ibid., fragment 10 (p. 80, lines 26–27).

49. Ibid., fragment 13A (p. 88, lines 20–23).

50. Ibid., fragment 21 (p. 128, line 5).

51. Ibid., fragment 12 (p. 86, lines 9–10).

52. *1 Clement* 47:1–3.

53. Grant and Graham, *First and Second Clement*, 65.

54. This is rightly emphasized by C. Eggenberger, *Die Quellen der politischen Ethik des 1. Clemensbriefes* (Zurich: Zwingli, 1951), 19–41. On the content of the letter, see Horrell, *Social Ethos of the Corinthian Correspondence*, 272–78.

55. This is an expansion of Isaiah 3:5.

56. Eusebius, *Church History* 4.23; see also 2.25.8; 3.4.10.

57. Ibid. 2.25.8.

58. Nautin, *Lettres et écrivains chrétiens*, 13–32.

59. When Origen contrasted the *ecclesiae* of cities with those of churches, he had their behavior in mind, not their structure (*Against Celsus* 3.29–30).

60. R. Cagnat, *Inscriptiones Graecae ad Res Romanas pertinentes* (Paris, Leroux, 1906), 3.88. An earlier high priest of "the heavenly god Augustus" at Amastris is named in ILS 5883.

61. Lucian, *Alexander* 25, cited by Cagnat, *Inscriptiones Graecae*, 131.

62. Strabo describes Amastris briefly (12.3.10, pp. 544–45).

63. Basil, *On the Holy Spirit* (SC 17 bis, 511–13), cited by H. Crouzel, *Grégoire le Thaumaturge Remerciement à Origène* (SC 148, 26).

64. Pliny, *Epistles* 10.96.6. Note that *Epistles* 90–91 deal with Sinope, 92–93 with Amisus, and 98–99 with Amastris, all fairly close together.

Chapter 5. God and the Gods

1. Cf. LXX Deut. 32:17; Ps. 96:5; 106:37; plus apocryphal literature.

2. Pausanias 2.2–5; cf. Roux, *Pausanias en Corinthie*.

3. The goddess Isis appeared to Lucius near Cenchreae, according to Apuleius, *Metamorphoses* 10.35, 11.4.

4. Dinsmoor, "Largest Temple." Pausanias calls a smaller temple at Tegea the largest in the Peloponnesus (8.45.5).

5. Athenaeus 13.588C says that this goddess appeared to Lais at night "and revealed the coming of rich lovers."

6. Hammond suggests that "what Pausanias probably saw was her statue in the temple of the gens Julia" ("Octavia [Minor]," 1865). He follows Imhoff-Blumer and Gardner, "Numismatic Commentary on Pausanias," 71.

7. For the significant remains, see Pausanias, LCL V Plate 43.

8. Annual sacrifices were then established in their honor (given up after 146) and a figure of Terror (*Deima*) set up.

9. Pindar says she gave a bridle to the Corinthian hero Bellerophon for the winged horse Pegasus (*Olympian Odes* 13.64–82, where she is called Hippias).

10. See Smith, "Egyptian Cults of Corinth," 228–31; P. Bouneau, "Isis Pélagia," *BCH* 87 (1963): 301–8.

11. On the temple of Sarapis there, see Strabo, *Geography* 17.1.17, 801. Canopus was apparently the destination of the Roman discussed by Justin Martyr and in chapter 7 below.

12. See Stroud, "Sanctuary of Demeter and Kore"; *Corinth*, vol. 8, part 3. Pausanias as an initiate could have seen the images ("anyone who has been initiated at Eleusis or has read the so-called *Orphica* knows what I mean"; *Description of Greece* 1.37.4; cf. 38.7).

13. In fact, the epithet came from the hill (*bounos*) on which the temple stood.

14. Cf. the Platonized Isis of Plutarch, *On Isis* 372E–F; 374A–B; cf. also the discussion in P Oxy 11.1380.

15. For an inscription, see chapter 1.

16. Cf. Philo, *Creation* 45: men believe in phenomena rather than God.

148 Notes

17. Maximus of Tyre 2.10c–d, p. 29, lines 7–13 Deubner. I owe this reference to Ronne Hartfield.
18. Diodorus 1.83.6–9.
19. Philo, *Virtues* 125.
20. Philo, *Virtues* 140, 145–46. For Greek and Greco-Roman parallels, see Grant, *Early Christians and Animals*, 9.
21. Josephus, *Antiquities* 4.233.
22. Luke 14:5 relates that Jesus commended pulling an ox out of a well even on the Sabbath.
23. This idea is repeated in 1 Tim. 5:18: "The laborer deserves to be paid."
24. Cf. 1 Cor. 3:5–9 on Paul and Apollos as coworkers with or under God.
25. Philo, *Special Laws* 3.46; 4.204–5; cf. Philo, *Virtues* 146.
26. Josephus, *Antiquities* 4.228–29.
27. Aristeas 128–66 (birds 145–50, animals 163–66).
28. Ibid. 144.
29. H. Usener, *Epicurea* (Leipzig: Teubner, 1887), 78, line 10; for Stoics, see SVF 3:367–76.
30. Philo, *Special Laws* 1.260.
31. Cf. Rom.1:23: "images resembling a mortal human being or birds or four-footed animals or reptiles."
32. Cf. 1 Thess. 4:14: "Jesus died and rose again."
33. Cf. the following "instructions we gave you through the Lord Jesus" (1 Thess. 4:2): "the will of God" on marriage (vv. 3–8); "taught by God to love one another" (v. 9); the word of the Lord on his coming (vv. 15–17); and "you know very well" about the day of the Lord coming "like a thief in the night" (5:2).
34. L. Crosby (*Dio Chrysostom* [LCL 5.163]) translates *panta en pasin* in *Oration* 71.1 as "in everything in any surroundings," but BAG notes that this has "a somewhat different coloring" (832). Compare the meanings of the similar expression *panta pasin*, which differs in 1 Cor. 9:22 ("all things to all people") and 10:33 ("everyone in everything").
35. Cf. R. M. Grant, "Chains of Being in Early Christianity," in *Christian Beginnings: Apocalypse to History* (London: Variorum, 1983), reprinted from *Myths and Symbols: Studies in Honor of Mircea Eliade*, ed. J. M. Kitagawa and C. H. Long (Chicago: University of Chicago Press, 1969), 279–89.
36. Philo, *Decalogue* 155.
37. He might better have said with Philo, "He who is truly God is one, but those improperly so-called are more" (*Dreams* 1.229).
38. See, however, Gal. 3:20; Betz, *Galatians*, 172–73.

Notes # 149

39. *Hermas, Mandate* 1.1; Theophilus 1.4; see also Philo, *Dreams* 1.63; Philo, *Flight* 75; Theophilus 2.3.7; 2.22.2.
40. Irenaeus, *Heresies* 4.20.2.
41. J. Dillon, *The Middle Platonists* (London: Duckworth, 1977), 162, citing Philo, *Abraham* 121; see also *Change of Names* 15–32.
42. R. M. Grant, *After the New Testament* (Philadelphia: Fortress, 1967), 113–16, reprinted from "Causation and the 'Ancient World-View,'" *JBL* 83 (1964): 34–40.
43. Marcus Aurelius 4.23.
44. Philo, *Cherubim* 125–26.

Chapter 6. Liturgy at Corinth

1. Apuleius, *Metamorphoses* 11.17; for other prayers, see G. Wissowa, *Religion und Kultus der Römer* (Munich: Beck, 1912), 83.
2. Lietzmann, *An die Korinther*, 82, gives other references, one to the Third Council of Carthage in 397: "It was agreed that the eucharist should not be given to dead bodies . . . and it was feared that the weakness of brothers might believe that the dead can be baptized."
3. The rock was at Rephidim, near the wilderness of Sinai, in Exodus 17, or at Kadesh, north of the wilderness of Zin, in Numbers 20.
4. Cf. Justin, *Apology* 1.66.3: "Do this for my remembrance, this is my body."
5. RSV paraphrases as "guilty of profaning."
6. Diogenes Laertius 6.39.
7. Celsus, *Medicine* 3.18.2.
8. 1 Cor. 12:3: "No one can say 'Jesus is Lord' except by the Holy Spirit."
9. Josephus, *Antiquities* 18.117. First Peter 3:21 opposes this view: "not as a removal of dirt from the body."
10. Cited in Epiphanius, *Heresies* 30.13.
11. Cited in Jerome, *Against Pelagius* 3.2.
12. See, for example, the table in Lietzmann, *An die Korinther*, 59.
13. Acts 20:7: "On the first day of the week, when we met to break bread . . ." Conzelmann, (*Apostelgeschichte*, 115), guts the story and calls its remaining essence "secular with popular-comic elements." He also treats 27:35 as an interpolation, while rightly denying that it is "the celebration of a eucharist" (145).
14. Mark 6:35–44 (8:1–10); Matt. 14:13–21 (15:32–39); Luke 9:12–17.
15. Cicero, *Laws* 2.37; Livy 39.8–19.
16. Livy 39.8.3, 6.

17. Livy 39.18.3–4.
18. Ibid. 39.13.8–14.
19. Ibid. 39.9.4, 10.7.
20. Ibid. 39.13.12 (with note by E. T. Sage, *Livy* 11 [LCL], 254, n. 1); compare the chemical knowledge of the Marcosians (Hippolytus, *Refutation of All Heresies* 6.30.3–4).
21. Livy 39.18.8–9.
22. ILS 18.
23. Cicero, *Laws* 2.37, cites the case as showing "the strictness of our ancestors."
24. Pliny, *Epistles* 10.97.2: *conquirendi non sunt*; Livy 39.14.7: priests *conquiri*.
25. Livy 39.18.3–4; cf. 8.6–8. Crimes against property were important at all stages of the case.
26. Presumably this kind of *carmen* was more like a soldiers' song about their commander, as in Livy 39.7.3.
27. Cf. Lietzmann, *Messe und Herrenmahl*, 230–38; M. Weinfeld, "Grace after Meals in Qumran," *JBL* 111 (1992): 427–40, esp. 436–37.
28. The catechetical instruction in *Didache* 1—5.
29. "Kingdom" is omitted as in the Sahidic version of Matthew and in the eucharistic thanksgiving below.
30. *Didache* 7—8 are echoed in *Apostolic Constitutions* 7.22–24.
31. Jesus is called *pais* in liturgical language in *1 Clem.* 59.2–61.3; Acts 3:13, 26; 4:27, 30; *Didache* 9.2–3; 10.1; *Martyrdom of Polycarp* 14.1, 3; Hippolytus, *Apostolic Tradition* 3–4.1.
32. *Didache* 9.1–5 is revised in *Apostolic Constitutions* 7.26.1–2.
33. Later eucharistic prayers expand this sentence.
34. *Didache* 10.2–3 is echoed in *Apostolic Constitutions* 7.26.1–2. Food, drink, and eternal life appear in John 6:53–54.
35. *Didache* 10.5 is echoed in *Apostolic Constitutions* 7.26.4, 27.2.
36. This line is omitted from *Apostolic Constitutions* 7.25.5–6, which reads: "Maranatha; Hosanna to the Son of David; blessed is he who comes in the name of the Lord, the Lord God manifest to us in flesh. If anyone is holy, let him come. If anyone is not, let him become so through repentance."
37. This follows the Bryennius manuscript. Various editors emend to "Son" with *Apostolic Constitutions* 7.26.5.
38. The passage is revised in *Apostolic Constitutions* 7.16.5–6. *Marana tha* means, "Our Lord, come"; cf. 1 Cor. 16:22; Rev. 22:16–17, 20.
39. This section appears only in *Apostolic Constitutions* 7.27 and the Coptic version. Cf. *Apostolic Constitutions* 7.22.2: "First you will anoint with holy oil, then baptize with water, and finally seal

with myrrh, so that the anointing will be participation in the Holy Spirit, the water symbol of death, and the myrrh seal of the covenants."

40. *Apostolic Constitutions* 7.26.6 reads, "But allow your presbyters also to give thanks," thus modernizing completely.

41. Justin too treats eucharistic prayers as sacrifices (*Dial.* 117.1–2); cf. Irenaeus, *Heresies* 4.17–19.

42. This theme was rightly emphasized by C. Eggenberger, *Die Quellen der politischen Ethik des 1. Klemensbriefes* (Zürich: Zwingli, 1951), 19–41.

43. R. Knopf, *Die Lehre der Zwölf Apostel/Die Zwei Clemensbriefe* (Tübingen: Mohr (Siebeck), 1920), 76–77; see also Eggenberger, *Quellen der politischen Ethik*, 87–104. On the content, see Horrell, *Social Ethos*, 255–56.

44. This theme is discussed by rhetoricians; cf. the elder Seneca, *Suasoria* 1; Quintilian 3.8.16.

45. On breasts, see Philo, *On the Creation* 38, 133; cf. W. Jaeger, "Echo eines unbekannten Tragikerfragments in Clemens' Brief an die Korinther," *Rheinisches Museum* 102 (1959): 330–40. *Eternity of the World* 66 rejects the figure of speech as "silly"; cf. D. T. Runia, *Philo in Early Christian Literature* (Minneapolis: Fortress, 1993), 88.

46. The doxology is paralleled in *1 Clement* 59.1–61.3.

47. Tertullian, *Apology* 30.4 (citing 1 Tim. 2:2). On prayer for emperors, see Justin, *Apology* 1.17.3 (sober mind); Athenagoras, *Embassy* 27.3 (orderly succession, also 1 Tim. 2:2); Theophilus 1.11 (honor through prayer). The tradition begins with Romans 13.

48. Josephus, *War* 2.409–10; cf. Josephus, *Against Apion* 2.76–77 (Jews instituted sacrifices and pay for them); Philo, *Embassy* 157, 317 (emperors instituted and pay).

49. Ignatius, *Ephesians* 12.2; 13.1; 20.2 (with the breaking of the bread as in Luke 24:35 and Acts 2:42); Ignatius, *Romans* 6.3.

50. Ignatius, *Philadelphians* 4; Ignatius, *Smyrnaeans* 7.1.

51. Ignatius, *Ephesians* 3.2; Ignatius, *Smyrnaeans* 8.1–2; *Didache* 10.7–13.7; 15.1–2.

52. Ignatius, *Trallians* 7.2; Ignatius, *Ephesians* 5.2–3; *Didache* 9.5.

53. Ignatius, *Polycarp* 6.2.

54. Ignatius, *Smyrnaeans* 1.1; Ignatius, *Ephesians* 18.2.

Chapter 7. Rites in the Second Century

1. Cf. the similar language in Musonius, fragment 6, p. 52, lines 41–32 Lutz: "People who undertake philosophy have been born in corruption and filled with depravity and evil" and p. 54, lines

35–37: "Depravity in us straight from childhood, and evil behavior derived from the depravity." Cf. also Plato, *Republic* 461B: a child "born under darkness with evil incontinence."

2. Cf. Heb. 6:4; 10:32; Eph. 5:14 "Sleeper awake! Rise from the dead, and Christ will shine on you."

3. Exodus 3:5 is supposedly the source of pagan customs (62.3–4), discussed, for example, in Porphyry, *On Abstinence* 2.46, p. 174, line 22 Nauck. Justin then digresses to Christ in the Old Testament (63). C. I. K. Story's claim ("Justin's Apology I.62–64," 177–78) that this chapter contains "no real digression but . . . an important continuation to Justin's argument" neglects the arrangement of the chapters on liturgy.

4. This resembles what Justin's older contemporary Numenius said about Naiad nymphs presiding over waters, also with a reference to Gen. 1:2 (fragment 30 in Des Places).

5. The Orphic literature discussed the birth of Athena (fragments 174 and 176 in Kern) and associated Koré with Athena as creator-figures (fragments 178 and 180). On Athena as *phronésis*, see F. Buffière, *Les mythes d'Homère et la pensée grecque* (Paris: Belles Lettres, 1956), 279–89.

6. Justin, *Apology* 1.26.2. Tertullian, *Apology* 13.9 tries to improve by citing it as *Sancti Dei*.

7. ILS 3472–74. Inscription 3472 is on display in the Vatican Museum.

8. Tertullian, *Baptism* 5.1; cf. A. D. Nock, "Pagan Baptisms in Tertullian."

9. The title *proestôs* ("presiding officer") appears twice in Hippolytus's *Commentary on Daniel* in reference to unnamed leaders from unnamed towns in remote Syria and Pontus (4.18.2, 19.1). It has a longer history at Rome, beginnning as a participle (*proistamenoi*) referring to presbyters in the *Shepherd of Hermas* (perhaps after 1 Tim. 5:17, *proestôtes presbuteroi*), continuing with a single *proestôs* in Justin, and twice in Irenaeus (plural). At Alexandria, Clement speaks of heretical leaders who "preside over a school rather than a church" (*Miscellanies* 7.92.7), and Origen denounces such *proestékotes* as unworthy presbyters, deacons, and bishops (*Commentary on Matthew* 10.22). For *proestôs* as "ruler," see Jalland, "Justin Martyr and the President"; for evidence from pagan authors, see LXX, Irenaeus, *Heresies* 1.10.2; Eusebius, *Church History* 4.23.2; 5.24.9; 6.20.2; 8.6.6; also Socrates, *Church History* 3.7. For deacons as eucharistic assistants, see Ignatius, *Trallians* 2.3.

10. Cf. Colson, "Notes on Justin Martyr," 166–68, with references to Galen.

11. This is excerpted largely from Luke 22:19–20.

12. Tertullian does not make this point but in *Baptism* 5.1 speaks of washings in initiations to Isis and Mithras and in *Crown* 15.3–4 gives further details about initiation.

13. Cited by Porphyry, *On Abstinence* 2.56, p. 181, 3 Nauck; 4.16, p. 254, 12. See discussion by O. Seel, "Pallas (2)," RE 18.3 (1983): 239–43.

14. In the New Testament, Sunday is called the first day of the week or after the Sabbath (Mark 16:9). *Barnabas* (15.9) calls it the eighth day, Ignatius the Lord's day (cf. Rev. 1:10). Justin does not use either term for it, conceivably aware of Greco-Egyptian references to "imperial [*sebasté*] day"; cf. A. Deissmann, *Light from the Ancient East*, new ed. (New York: Doran, 1927), 358–60.

15. In the New Testament, as in the *Martyrdom of Polycarp* (7.1) and Hippolytus, *Apostolic Tradition* 20.7, Friday is called *paraskeué* or "preparation" (for the Sabbath). The *Didache* (8.1) too follows Jewish practice by counting days in relation to the Sabbath. Justin, like the apologists after him, follows the "comparatively recent" planetary week used by Romans (Dio Cassius 37.17.3–19.3) but may prefer not to mention Venus Day (criticizing the goddess in *Apology* 1.25.1). See Colson, "Notes on Justin Martyr," 169–71.

16. Justin, *Dialogue* 41.1.

17. Justin, *Apology* 1.65.2.

18. 1 Cor. 16:20; 2 Cor. 13:12; 1 Thess. 5:26, Rom. 16:16; cf. *Apostolic Constitutions* 2.57.17; 8.11.7–10.

19. See G. W. H. Lampe, *A Patristic Greek Lexicon* (Oxford: Clarendon, 1968), s.v. *eiréné*.

20. For criticism of such syntheses, especially those of K. M. Hofmann (*Philema hagion* [Gütersloh: Bertelsmann, 1938]), see Thraede, "Ursprunge und Formen des 'Heiligen Küsses'"; Thraede, "Friedenskuss."

21. *Questions on Exodus* 2.78, 118; Aucher, *Philonis Judaei paralipomena armena*, 522, 545. Philo really refers to "the [cosmic] embrace of concord" (2.78, p. 128 in Marcus) and to "[cosmic] loving embrace" (2.118, p. 169) and does not mention literal kisses. Marcus rightly claims that the previous *Questions on Exodus* 2.117 (p. 544 in Aucher, p. 168 in Marcus) is largely Christian.

22. Conybeare, "Kiss of Peace." He supplies his own Greek, not found in the editions of Aucher or F. Petit, *Quaestiones in Genesim et in Exodum: fragmenta graeca* (Paris: Cerf, 1978).

23. H. Windisch, *Der zweite Korintherbrief* (Göttingen: Vandenhoek & Ruprecht, 1924), 427; followed by Hofmann, *Philema hagion*, 126.

24. The Greek version can be found in C. Burchard, *Gesammelte Studien zu Joseph und Asenath*, Studia in Veteris Testamenti Pseudepigrapha 13 (1996): 192. For an English translation, see J. H. Charlesworth, ed., *The Old Testament Pseudepigrapha* (Garden City, N.Y.: Doubleday, 1985), 177–247.

25. Cf. the restrictions of *Joseph and Asenath* 8.5–7, (pp. 170–71 in Burchard, p. 271 in Charlesworth).

26. Athenagoras, *Embassy* 32.5.

27. Clement, *Tutor* 3.81.2–4.

28. Hippolytus, *Apostolic Tradition* 18.3–5.

29. Ignatius, *Philadelphians* 7.1.

30. Irenaeus, *Against Heresies* 1.13.3.

31. *Secundum suam potestatem*, Hippolytus, *Apostolic Tradition* 10.4; cf. Justin, *Apology* 1.67.5.

32. The discussion of Melito and Theophilus is taken from my essay, "The Structure of Eucharistic Prayers," *Antiquity and Humanity: Essays on Ancient Religion and Philosophy Presented to Hans Dieter Betz on His 70th Birthday*, ed. A. Y. Collins and M. M. Mitchell (Tübingen: Mohr, 2001), 321–32. On both authors, cf. L. Pernot, *La rhétorique de l'éloge dans le monde gréco-romain* (Paris: Institut d'Études Augustiniennes, 1993), 776.

33. Cited by Jerome, *Illustrious Men* 24.

34. Printed in E. J. Goodspeed, *Die ältesten Apologeten* (Göttingen: Vandenhoeck & Ruprecht, 1914), 310–11; O. Perler, *Méliton de Sardes*, SC 123 (Paris: Cerf, 1966), 228–33 (especially parallels from Zeno of Verona); S. G. Hall, *Melito of Sardis On Pascha and Fragments* (Oxford: Clarendon, 1979), 70–73 ("doubtfully authentic," xxxii).

35. In 1950, I emphasized the philosophical connections of Melito's rhetoric ("Melito of Sardis On Baptism," *VC* 4 [1950]: 33–36), but rhetoric is considerably more important.

36. For the Stoics, the Nile was a prime example of divine providence; cf. Cicero, *Nature of the Gods* 2.130.

37. Perler, *Méliton*, 228–29n3; cf. Theophilus 2.13.

38. Compare "ocean uncrossable by men" in *1 Clement* 20.8.

39. Cf. Pernot, *Rhétorique de l'èloge dans*, 779–80; the "more marvelous sight" in Theophilus 1.13.

40. Marcion rejected the gospel account of Jesus' baptism and passed from Luke 3:1 to 4:34. Harnack, *Marcion: das Evangelium vom fremden Gott* (TU 45, ed.2, 1924), 183*.

41. Harnack, *Marcion*, 421*-23*, refers to the fragment as a "ganz rhetorisch und daher echt kleinasiatische Fragment." A better proof is given by the unction text of Theophilus.

42. Theophilus (1.12) derives "Christian" from "unction," and similarly Justin (*Apology* 2.6.3) derives "Christ" from God's having "anointed and adorned everything through him," while according to Hippolytus (*Daniel Commentary* 4.30.8), Old Testament kings and priests are called *christoi* (not *christianoi*) because they are anointed with the holy oil that Moses prepared.

43. On pitch for ships, see Pliny *Natural History* 16.56,158; on houses, 36.166; on statues, 34.15 = 35.182. An anonymous text translated by D. A. Russell and N. G. Wilson, *Menander Rhetor* (Oxford: Clarendon, 1981), 364, calls the olive "specially appropriate to the competitors—gymnastic exercise involves the use of olive-oil."

44. Melito had said the air was washed.

45. Theophilus, 2.16. A different picture appears in Clement of Alexandria: "Oil lubricates the skin and relaxes the nerves and removes any heavy smell from the body. . . . Ointment is for use as a medicine and an aid to arouse lost strength, and for catarrhs and colds." (*Tutor* 2.67.2, 68.2). He does not mention oil with baptism. For Gnostic unction "with white ointment from the tree of life," see Origen, *Against Celsus* 6.27, with Chadwick's note (342n2).

46. Theophilus, cf. *Apostolic Constitutions* 7.42.3: "that he may consecrate the oil in the name of the Lord Jesus and give spiritual grace and effective power, the remission of sins and the preparation for the confession of baptism, so that the one anointed, freed from all impiety, may become worthy of initiation after the command of the Only-begotten."

47. Jerome, *Illustrious Men* 24 cites Tertullian for Melito's *elegans et declamatorium ingenium*.

48. Tertullian, *On Baptism* 3.6.

49. So argue R. F. Refoulé and M. Drouzy, *Tertullien Traité de baptême*, SC 35 (Paris: Cerf, 1952), 68n2.

50. Tertullian, *Against Marcion* 1.14.3, cited by Harnack, *Marcion*, 144. Unction appears in *On Baptism* 7.1–2: *nobis carnaliter currit unctio sed spiritaliter proficit*.

51. Jerome relies on Tertullian when discussing *aquarum laudes* "from the rhetorical school" (*Epistle* 69 [PL 22.659B; cf. 654A]), but uses only biblical examples.

52. The versions of B. S. Easton (1934) and G. Dix (1937) have been superseded by the basic text of Botte, *La Tradition Apostolique de saint Hippolyte* (1963).

53. J. R. Srawley, *The Early History of the Liturgy* (Cambridge, Mass.: Cambridge University Press, 1947), 166. For our purposes it

makes no difference whether "Hippolytus" is a person or a group.

54. Hippolytus, *Apostolic Tradition* 4.4–13.
55. Lietzmann, *Messe und Herrenmahl*, 176 (E.T. 143); cf. A. Hamann in *Encyclopedia of the Early Church* 293 (a).

Chapter 8. Christian Conduct

1. Ulpian, *Epitome* 16.1; cf. Kunkel, "Matrimonium," 2268; Humbert, *Remariage à Rome*, 154–60; E. Bund, "Matrimonium," KP 3 (1969): 1081–83; E. M. Lassen, "The Roman Family: Ideal and Metaphor," in Moxnes, ed., *Constructing Early Christian Families*, 107–8.
2. Justin, *Apology* 1.15.6.
3. Cited in R. Walzer, *Galen on Jews and Christians* (London: Oxford University Press, 1949), 15–16, from a lost summary of Plato's *Republic*.
4. See, e.g., Soranus, *Gynecology* 1.30–32 (CMG 4.20–22); Galen, *Affected Places* 6.5 (8.417–20 in Kühn; included in selections by Oribasius, *Medical Collections* 6.37 [CMG 6.1.1]), Rufus of Ephesus (CMG 6.38). Continent men were supposedly taller and stronger (Soranus, *Gynecology* 1.30; A. Rousselle, *Porneia: On Desire and the Body in Antiquity*, trans. F. Pheasant [New York: Blackwell, 1988], 20).
5. D. Martin, "Paul without Passion," in Moxnes, ed., *Constructing Early Christian Families*, 201–15.
6. Justin, *Apology* 1.29.1, in agreement with Soranus, *Gynecology* 1.32 (CMG 4.21, 23); Musonius fragment 12, p. 86, line 6 Lutz.
7. Cf. Osiek, *Shepherd of Hermas*, 42–45.
8. Justin, *Apology* 1.27.4. Cf. K. Schneider, "Meretrix," in RE 15.1021; F. Augar, "Die Frau im römischen Christenprocess," TU, Neue Folge N.F.13.4 (1905), 77 (pagan example = daughter of Sejanus, Dio 58.11.5; cf. Suetonius, *Tiberius* 61.5). Cf. P Oxy 3.528.
9. Tertullian, *Apology* 39.12. Socrates was supposed to have had a second wife, Myrto, for childbearing (Diogenes Laertius 2.26); for the story about Cato see below.
10. E. H. Warmington, *Remains of Old Latin* (LCL, 1938), 78–79. Cicero, *Letters to Friends* 7.24.1 (45 B.C.): "It was Cipius, I think, who said, 'I am not asleep to everyone.'"
11. Plutarch, *Marital Counsel* 16–17, 140B–C; cf. Plutarch, *Dialogue on Love* 759F–760A.
12. Ovid, *Loves* 2.19.47–48; 57. Cf. Martial 1.73; 3.70.
13. Juvenal 1.55–57; 9.70–80.

14. Apuleius, *Apology* 75. For the theme of "payment from wife's adulterers," see Alciphron, *Letters of Parasites* 26.4.
15. P Oxy 3.528.
16. Clement, *Miscellanies* 3.25.6.
17. Epiphanius, *Heresies* 25.1.5; 26.4.1–2.
18. Cf. Paul's counsel in 1 Cor. 7:5; Weiss, *Erste Korintherbrief* 171–76, with his reference to Chrysostom, *Homily* 19.1, on 1 Corinthians (PG 61.152–53): "great evils arise from this kind of continence; for often adulteries, fornications, and changes of homes come from it. What is the gain from fasting and continence if love is torn asunder? None. How many reproaches, how many court cases, how much war must arise from this?"
19. Origen, *Commentary on Matthew* 14.24, p.344 Klostermann; similarly in *Homilies on 1 Corinthians* (C. Jenkins "Origin on 1 Corinthians," *JTS* 9 [1907–8]: 500–501). See H. Crouzel, *Virginité et mariage selon Origène* (Paris and Bruges: Desclée de Brouwer, 1963), 166.
20. *Digest* 48.5.30.4.
21. See Rousselle, *Porneia*, 107–28.
22. Minucius Felix 9.5.
23. Thus, Justin (*Apology* 1.26.7) adds "eating human flesh" to "the overturning of the lamp and promiscuous sex."
24. Galen, *Temperament and Force of Simple Drugs* 10.1 (12.248 in Kühn).
25. Tertullian, *Apology* 9.2.
26. Ignatius uses Paul's language to call himself "the least of them and an abortion" (*Rom*. 9.2); he also says that "my birth is imminent" (6.1) and expects to "become a man" (6.2). "Abortion" implies "incomplete" and probably "premature."
27. See J. T. Noonan Jr., *Contraception* (Cambridge, Mass.: Belknap Press, 1965), 9–139.
28. See J. H. Waszink, "Abtreibung," *RAC* 1 (1950), 55–60.
29. CMG 1.1, p. 4, lines 16–17. A Christian version in a tenth-century manuscript reads thus: "I will not give women an abortive above or below."
30. W. Dittenberger, *Sylloge Inscriptionum Graecarum*, 3d ed., no. 985, line 21.
31. Musonius, fragment 15 (p. 96 in Lutz); cf. K. Hopkins, "A Textual Emendation in a Fragment of Musonius Rufus: A Note on Contraception," *Classical Quarterly* 69 (1965): 72–74.
32. Plutarch, *Advice about Keeping Well* 22, 134F.
33. *Romulus* 22.3.
34. *Lycurgus* 3.2.

35. Soranus, *Gynecology* 1.60–63 (CMG 4.45–47), including *pityos phloion*, 62. Cf. Caelius Aurelianus, *Gynecology*, ed. M. F. and I. E. Drabkin, Supplements to the Bulletin of the History of Medicine 13 (Baltimore: Johns Hopkins, 1951), 28–30 (1.82–85).
36. Soranus, *Gynecology* 1.64–65 (CMG 4.47–49).
37. Theon, *Progymnasmata* 2, p. 69, 7–10 Spengel.
38. Philo, *Special Laws* 3.108–9, 111, 117–18.
39. Eusebius, *Gospel Preparation* 8.7.7 = LCL *Philo* 9.428–29.
40. Josephus, *Against Apion* 2.202.
41. *Didache* 2.2; *Barnabas* 19.5; *Apostolic Constitutions* 7.3.2.
42. *Apocalypse of Peter* 8 (Ethiopic), 26 (Greek); *Apocalypse of Paul* 40: abortion punished in hell.
43. Athenagoras, *Embassy* 33.1–2; 35.6.
44. Clement, *Tutor* 2.95.3.
45. Ibid. 2.96.1.
46. Clement, *Prophetic Selections* 48.1–50.3.
47. Tertullian, *Apology* 9.8. Cf. Martial: "What you lose with your fingers, Ponticus, is a man" (9.41.10).
48. Tertullian, *Exhortation to Chastity* 12.5.
49. Tertullian, *On the Soul* 25.5 (= SVF 2.805); cf. 37.2.
50. J. H. Waszink, *Tertullian De Anima* (Amsterdam: Meulenhoff, 1947), 336.
51. Aulus Gellius, *Attic Nights* 12.1.8–9; cf. Ulpian, in *Digest* 48.8.8: If a woman uses force against her inner parts in order to procure abortion, the provincial governor should drive her into exile.
52. *Digest* 48.19.38.5, vol. 2, p. 853 Mommsen.

Chapter 9. Marital Problems

1. Aristotle, *Nicomachean Ethics* 8.10.5; cf. 11.4, 12.7.
2. Aristotle, *Politics* 7.14.
3. Appian, *Syrian War* 59–61; Plutarch, *Demetrius* 38; Lucian, *Syrian Goddess* 17–19 ("romanhaft ausgeschmückt," H. Volkmann, KP 5 [1975], 394).
4. Julian, *Misopogon* 347A–348A, modified from Plutarch.
5. Plutarch, *Life of Cato* 25 (Plutarch finds the case problematic); see also C.52. Seneca says "Marcia ran between Hortensius and Cato" (*On Matrimony*, fragment 74 in the edition of Haase).
6. On the account, see Humbert, *Remariage à Rome*, 97–99.
7. Plutarch often refers to Stoics who influenced Cato (*Life of Cato* 4.1–2; 10.1–2; 16.1; 55.5) and his use of their paradoxes (21.5; 67.1–2). Like Plato, Stoics opposed monogamy (Diogenes Laertius 7.131).
8. Plutarch, *Life of Cato* 68.2; Plato, *Republic* 5.459D–E.
9. Seneca, *Controversies* 6.7.

10. Gaius, *Institutes* 1.63. Later authors reiterate: cf. *Collation of Mosaic and Roman Laws* 6 in *Fontes Iuris Romani Antejustiniani* 2, ed. S. Riccobono et al. (Florence: Barbera, 1940), 556–61.
11. Dio Chrysostom, *Orations* 30.19.
12. Cited in Lietzmann, *An die Korinther I–II*, 173.
13. Diogenes Laertius 6.69 (supposedly an Athenian virtue).
14. Sextus Empiricus, *Pyrrhonian Outlines* 3.205.
15. See E. M. Lassen, "The Roman Family: Ideal and Metaphor," in Moxnes, ed., *Constructing Early Christian Families* 107–8.
16. Horace, *Odes* 3.6.25–32; G. W. Williams, "Horatius Flaccus," *Oxford Classical Dictionary* 2nd ed. (Oxford: Clarendon, 1970), 528–29.
17. Suetonius, *Augustus* 89.2.
18. Dio Cassius 56.1–10.
19. Suetonius, *Claudius* 19; Seutonius, *Nero* 10.1.
20. Dio 54.16.6.
21. *Hunc divitem . . . divus Augustus indignum vindicta iudicavit . . . et tantum non pronuntiavit iure caesum videri* (Seneca, *Natural Questions* 1.16 [1.17, moral meditations]). Glass mirrors already existed (Pliny, *Natural History* 36.193 [cf. 196]), though perhaps metal would have sufficed.
22. Suetonius, *Augustus* 45.4.
23. Galen, *On Prognosis to Epigenes* 6 (14.631–33 in Kühn). For a case of "burning" supposedly not diagnosed by physicians, see Apuleius, *Metamorphoses* 10.2.
24. For Augustus, see K. Gelinsky, "Augustus' Legislation on Morals and Marriage," *Philologus* 125 (1981): 126–44; des Bouvrie, "Augustus' Legislation on Morals."
25. Suetonius, *Tiberius* 35.2.
26. Tacitus, *Annals* 2.85; cf. E. Meyer, "Seriphos," KP 5 (1975): 137.
27. Juvenal 6.489 mentions *Isiacae sacraria lenae*.
28. Josephus, *Antiquities* 18.66–73; for Isis, Anubis, and assignations, see Juvenal 6.489, 526–41. Two papyrus letters from Oxyrhynchus contain parallels to this part of the story. One is an invitation to "the banquet of the Lord Sarapis in the temple of Thoeris" (P Oxy 12.1484). In the other, an absent husband informs his wife that he has offered worship twice a day "before Thoeris who loves you" (3.528). Thoeris, sometimes identified with Athena, was prominent at Oxyrhynchus (W. Helck, "Thoeris," KP 5 [1975]: 771).
29. Josephus, *Antiquities* 18.74–80.
30. Corbett, *Roman Law of Marriage*, 143.
31. Josephus, *Antiquities* 18.81–84; Tacitus, *Annals* 2.84; Suetonius, *Tiberius* 36.

32. Suetonius, *Gaius* 40–41.
33. Juvenal 6.116–32; cf. Highet, *Juvenal the Satirist*, 164–68.
34. See Highet, *Juvenal the Satirist*, 91–103, 269.
35. Cf. Humbert, *Remariage à Rome*, 76–112 ("La fréquence des mariages," rivaling Hollywood).
36. Tacitus, *Annals* 12.5–9.
37. For his 300 million sesterces, see Dio 61.10.3 (cf. 62.2.1).
38. Tacitus, *Annals* 12.53.
39. Ibid. 14.63–64.
40. Ibid. 16.19–20.
41. Suetonius, *Domitian* 8.3–4.
42. For a random example of a Corinthian's concern, see Oribasius, *Medical Collections* 6.38 (CMG 6.1.1): Rufus of Ephesus prescribed a liquid diet for a man from Corinth unable to ejaculate.
43. Cf. the Cynic Diogenes (Diogenes Laertius 6.46; more fully in Dio Chrysostom 6.16–20) and the Stoic Zeno (Sextus Empiricus, *Pyrrhonian Outlines* 3.206 [SVF 1.255]). Chrysippus seems to have accepted prostitution (SVF 3.755–56) but not keeping a brothel (3.152). On food and sex as natural, see Aristotle, *Nicomachean Ethics* 3.11.1.
44. SVF 3.149–50; 3.289.
45. Musonius, fragment 12 (p. 86, line 24–27 Lutz); Clement, *Tutor* 2.100; Epictetus 4.5.10; Marcus Aurelius 8.55; H. Cherniss (*Plutarch's Moralia* 17.2, LCL 1976), 479n.
46. Weiss, *Erste Korintherbrief*, 165.
47. Lietzmann, *An die Korinther I–II*, 28.
48. Here Paul uses *allassô* and compounds to point toward unnatural changes (Rom. 1:23, 25, 26).
49. Cf. "better to marry than to be aflame with passion," (1 Cor. 7:9).
50. *Aschémosuné*; cf. *sumplokas aschémonas* in Musonius, fragment 12, p. 86, line 3 Lutz.
51. Cf. Plato, *Laws* 1.636C: "When males unite with females for procreation the pleasure is held to be due to nature, but when males with males or females with females, contrary to nature."
52. Athenaeus 13.605D ("Aphrodite"); Appian, *Civil Wars* 1.109 (rape), Diodorus Siculus 11.1; 32.10.9 (intercourse with hermaphrodites, marriage); Philo, *Special Laws* 3.39 (pleasure); Josephus, *Against Apion* 2.273 (male intercourse); Musonius, fragment 12, p. 86, line 10 Lutz (male intercourse); Plutarch, *On Love* 751C, E (male intercourse). (Most of these references come from BAG 869.)
53. Cf. "It is not good that the man should be alone" (Gen. 2:18).
54. Cf. "bone of my bones and flesh of my flesh"; "out of Man this one was taken" (Gen. 2:23).

55. This corrects Gen. 4:1, where Eve says, "I have produced a man with the help of the LORD."

56. Josephus, *Against Apion* 2.201. B. Niese, an older editor, recalling Eph. 5:22 ("Wives, be subject to your husbands as you are to the Lord"), thought the statement was Christian.

57. See Betz, *Galatians*, 181–201, esp. 195–200; Grant, "Neither Male nor Female."

58. Philo, *Creation of the World* 76, 134.

59. Betz, *Galatians*, 200.

60. Cf. W. C. Van Unnik, "Studies over de zogenaande eerste brief van Clemens 1. Het litteraire genre," Mededelingen der Koninklijke Nederlander Akademie van Wetenschappen, Nieuwe Reaks 33.4 (1970), 160–62.

61. Tacitus, *Annals* 15.44.

62. "Happier" is too secular a translation for *makariôtera*.

63. Musonius, fragment 13A, p. 88, lines 13–14 Lutz; fragment 14, p. 94, lines 8–9; cf. van Geytenbeek, *Musonius Rufus and Greek Diatribe*, 65.

64. Antipater in SVF III, p. 255, lines 14–18 = Stobaeus, *Eclogues* 4.22.25, p. 508, lines 15–17 Hense.

65. See, e.g., Plutarch, *Marital Precepts* 20 (140D–F), 34 (142E–143A).

66. Hierocles in Stobaeus, *Eclogues* 4.22.1, p. 505, lines 14–16 Hense.

67. See Iamblichus, *Pythagorean Life* 167–68 (pp. 94–95 in Deubner); Acts 4:32 (cf. 2:44). Both expressions are proverbial according to Aristotle, *Nicomachean Ethics* 9.8.2.

68. See L. Mitteis and U. Wilcken, *Grundzüge und Chrestomathie der Papyruskunde* 2.2 (Leipzig and Berlin: Teubner, 1912), nos. 283–87; A. S. Hunt and C. C. Edgar, *Select Papyri* 1 (LCL, 1932), nos. 1–5.

69. Mishnah: *Ketuboth* 5.6, p. 252 Danby; Plutarch, *Life of Solon* 20.3; Plutarch, *On Love* 769A.

70. *Hermas, Mandates* 4.1.5–9; Osiek, *Shepherd of Hermas*, 110–12.

71. The terms are traditionally Stoic. For right reason, see SVF 3.445 from Clement, *Tutor* (everything contrary to right reason is sin); SVF 4.100a–b (right reason is law of nature); SVF 4.41b–42a; 3.308–13 (right is what is right).

72. Doubtless she supposed he had visited Canopus, just east of Alexandria, which was notorious for "Canopism," shamelessness and the ultimate in license (Strabo, *Geography* 17.1.16–17). On Nero (for example) and Alexandria, see A. J. Woodman, *Tacitus Reviewed* (Oxford: Clarendon, 1998), 180–88.

73. Justin, *Apology* 2.2. Cf. "A Woman of Rome," *Church History* 54

(1985), 461–72; *Greek Apologists of the Second Century* (Philadelphia: Westminster, 1988), 69–72.

74. Tacitus, *Annals* 12.53; cf. Gaius, *Institutes* 1.84 on offspring.

75. Suetonius, *Vespasian* 11.

76. Josephus, *Against Apion* 1.32; cf. 2.200.

77. Soranus, *Gynecology* 1.34 (CMG 4.23).

78. Musonius, fragment 13B, p. 90, lines 4–8 Lutz; cf. van Geytenbeek, *Musonius Rufus and Greek Diatribe*, 66.

79. Musonius, fragment 12 (pp. 86–88 in Lutz).

80. Hippolytus, *Refutation* 9.12.25 (contraceptives = *atokias pharmakois*).

81. Plutarch, *Marital Advice* 16.140B, though "a pleasure-loving husband makes his wife meretricious and licentious. . . . Many have shared their sexual pleasures, offering not only their girl friends but also their wives" (17.140C).

82. Plutarch, *Life of Marius* 38.3–4 (LCL 9.570–71).

83. Soranus, *Gynecology* 2.44 (CMG 4.85). When stipulating general requirements for a wet nurse, Soranus lists "chaste, sympathetic, calm, clean, Greek" (2.19; CMG 4.66).

84. In fact, he never uses the words *pais* or *brephos*, and he uses *paidion* only once. (He more frequently uses *népios*.)

85. 1 Cor. 13:10–11; 14:20 (do the Corinthians have something like Matt. 18:3 in mind?).

86. 1 Cor. 7:14. This is part of his discussion of mixed marriages between Christians and non-Christians in 1 Cor. 7:12–16.

87. See Harris, "Child-Exposure in the Roman Empire"; see also Philo, *Virtues* 131–33.

88. Tatian 28.3 imitates this passage.

89. Justin, *Apology* 1.27.1–4. Cf. 1.29.1; Athenagoras, *Embassy* 35.4 (murder); cf. the anonymous *To Diognetus* 5.6; Musonius, fragment 15 (pp. 96–101 in Lutz).

90. *1 Clement* 55.2; Theophilus 1.2. On the sale of children, see Taubenschlag, *Law of Greco-Roman Egypt*, 104.

91. Taubenschlag, *Law of Greco-Roman Egypt*, 55–56.

92. Tertullian, *To the Nations* 1.16.13–19. For the same Fuscianus's dealings with the Christian Callistus at Rome, see Hippolytus, *Refutation* 9.11.4; 12.7–10.

93. A father sells a son to a procurer in a "controversy" mentioned by Quintilian (7.1.55).

Bibliography

ABBREVIATIONS

AJA	*American Journal of Archaeology*
ASCSA	American School of Classical Studies at Athens
BAG	Bauer-Arndt-Gingrich, *A Greek-English Lexicon of the New Testament and Other Early Christian Literature*
BCH	*Bulletin de correspondance hellénique*
CMG	Corpus medicorum graecorum
CSEL	Corpus scriptorum ecclesiasticorum latinorum
CSHB	Corpus scriptorum historiae byzantinae
GCS	Griechischen christlichen Schriftsteller
HTR	*Harvard Theological Review*
IG	Inscriptiones Graecae
ILS	Inscriptiones Latinae Selectae
JAC	Jahrbuch für Antike und Christentum
JBL	*Journal of Biblical Literature*
JHS	*Journal of Hellenic Studies*
JTS	*Journal of Theological Studies*
KP	Der Kleine Pauly
LCL	Loeb Classical Library
LXX	Septuagint
NAG	Nachrichten von der Königlichen Gesellschaft der Wissenschaften zu Göttingen
OECT	Oxford Early Christian Texts
PG	Patrologia graeca (Migne)
PL	Patrologia latina (Migne)

| P Oxy | The Oxyrhynchus Papyri (Grenfell, Hunt, et al.) |

P Oxy   The Oxyrhynchus Papyri (Grenfell, Hunt, et al.)
PSI   Papiri della Società italiana per la ricerca dei Papiri (Vitelli, Norsa, et al.)
PTS   Patristische Texte und Studien
RAC   *Reallexikon für Antike und Christentum*
RE   Realencyclopèdie der classischen Altertumswissenschaft (Pauly-Wissowa)
SC   Sources chrétiennes
SVF   Stoicorum veterum fragmenta (von Arnim)
TU   Texte und Untersuchungen
VC   *Vigiliae christianae*
ZNW   *Zeitschrift für die neutestamentliche Wissenschaft*

TEXTS AND TRANSLATIONS

Aelius Aristides, vol. 1. Translated by C. A. Behr. LCL. 1973.
_____. vol. 2. Edited by B. Keil. Berlin: Weidmann, 1897.
Alciphron. *Epistulae*. Edited by M. A. Schepers. Leipzig: Teubner, 1905.
_____. *The Letters of Alciphron*. Translated by A. R. Benner and F. H. Fobes. LCL. 1949.
Apostolic Constitutions. Les Constitutions Apostoliques. Edited by M. Metzger. SC 320, 329, 336 (1985–1987).
Apostolic Fathers. *Die Apostolischen Väter*. Edited by K. Bihlmeyer and W. Schneemelcher. Part I. Tübingen: Mohr (Siebelle), 1956.
Barnabas. See Apostolic Fathers.
Celsus. *On Medicine*. Translated by W. G. Spencer. LCL. 1935-1938.
Chariton. Edited and translated by G. P. Goold. LCL. 1995.
Cicero. Various dates and editors, LCL.
Clement of Alexandria. Edited by O. Stählin. GCS 12, 15, 17, 39 (1905–1936).
Clement of Rome (1 Clement). See Apostolic Fathers.
Corinth. Vol. 1, part 1, *Introduction, Topography, Architecture*. By H. N. Fowler and R. Stillwell. Cambridge, Mass.: Harvard University Press, 1932.
_____. Vol. 1, part 3, *Monuments in the Lower Agora and North of the Lower Archaic Temple*. Edited by R. L. Scranton. Cambridge, Mass.: Harvard University Press, 1951.
_____. Vol. 1, part 4, *The South Stoa and Its Roman Successors*. Edited by O. Broneer. Princeton, N.J.: ASCSA, 1954.
_____. Vol. 3, part 1, *Acrocorinth*. Edited by C. W. Blegen et al. Cambridge, Mass.: Harvard University Press, 1930.

_____. Vol. 8, part 1, *Greek Inscriptions*. Edited by B. D. Meritt. Cambridge, Mass.: Harvard University Press, 1931.

_____. Vol. 8, part 2, *Latin Inscriptions*. Edited by A. B. West. Cambridge, Mass.: Harvard University Press, 1931.

_____. Vol. 8, part 3, *The Inscriptions, 1926–1950*. Edited by J. H. Kent. Cambridge, Mass.: Harvard University Press, 1966.

_____. Vol. 14, *The Asklepeion and Lerna*. Edited by C. Roebuck. Princeton, N.J.: ASCSA, 1951.

_____. Vol. 16, *Mediaeval Architecture in the Central Area of Corinth*. Edited by R. L. Scranton. Princeton, N.J.: ASCSA, 1957.

_____. Vol. 18, part 3, *The Sanctuary of Demeter and Kore: Topography and Architecture*. Edited by N. Boukidis and R. S. Stroud. Princeton, N.J.: ASCSA, 1997.

_____. Vol. 20. Edited by C. K. Williams and N. Bookides (Forthcoming).

De Usu partium. Edited by G. Helmreich. Vol. 2. Leipzig: Teubner, 1909.

Didache. See Apostolic Fathers.

Didascalia Apostolorum. Translated by R. H. Connolly. Oxford: Clarendon, 1929.

Didascalia et Constitutiones Apostolorum. Edited by F. X. Funk. Paderborn: Schoeningh, 1905.

Digest. *Digesta Iustiniani Augusti*. Edited by T. Mommsen, vol. 2. Berlin: Weidmann, 1870.

Dio Cassius. Translated by E. Cary. 9 vols. LCL, 1914–1927.

Dio Chrysostom. Translated by J. W. Cohoon et al. 5 vols. LCL, 1932–1951.

Epiphanius, *Against Heresies*. Edited by K. Holl. GCS 25, 31, 37 (1915–1933).

Eusebius. *La Préparation Évangélique*, Books 12–13. Edited by É. des Places. SC 307. 1983.

Firmicus Maternus. *Matheseos Libri VIII*. Vol. 1, edited by W. Kroll and F. Skutsch. Vol. 2, edited by W. Kroll, F. Skutsch, and K. Ziegler. Stuttgart: Teubner, 1968.

Galen. Edited by C. G. Kühn. 20 vols. Hildesheim: Olms, 1967.

Gaius. Institutionum Commentarii. Edited by E. Seckel and R. Kuehler. Leipzig: Teubner, 1908.

Georgios Phrantzes. *Chronicle*. Edited by I. Bekker. CSHB 36. Bonn: Weber, 1838.

Hermas, *Shepherd*. Edited by M. Whittaker, *Der Hirt des Hermas*. Berlin: Akademie, 1956.

Hippolytus. *Refutation of All Heresies*. Edited by P. Wendland. GCS 26. 1916. Edited by M. Marcovich. PTS 25. 1986.

Iamblichi. *De Vita Pythagorica Liber*. Edited by L. Deubner. Leipzig: Teubner, 1937.

Ignatius of Antioch. See Apostolic Fathers.

Inscriptiones Graecae, vol. 7. Edited by W. Dittenberger. Berlin: Reimer, 1892.

Irenaeus. *Contre les Hérésies*, vol. 1. Edited by A. Rousseau and L. Doutreleau. SC 263–26. 1979.

Justin Martyr. *Iustini Martyris Apologiae pro Christianis*. Edited by M. Marcovich. PTS 38. 1994.

_____. *Dialogus cum Tryphone*. PTS 47. 1997.

Liturgies Eastern and Western. Vol. 1. *Eastern Liturgies*, edited by F. E. Brightman. Oxford: Clarendon, 1896.

Livy. Vol. 11. Translated by E. T. Sage. LCL, 1936.

Lucian. 8 vols. Translated by A. M. Harmon et al. LCL. 1913–1967.

Musonius. Translated by C. Lutz. Yale Classical Studies 10, 1947.

Numenius. *Fragments*. Edited by E. Des Places. Paris: Belles Lettres, 1973.

Oribasius. *Collectionum Medicarum Reliquiae*, vol. 1. Edited by H. Raeder. CMG 6.1.1. Leipzig and Berlin: Teubner, 1928.

Orientis Graeci Inscriptiones Selectae. Edited by W. Dittenberger. Leipzig: Hirzel, 1905.

Orphicorum Fragmenta. Edited by O. Kern. Berlin: Weidmann, 1922.

Ovid. *Fasti*. Translated by J. G. Frazer. LCL. 1931.

Pausanias. *Description of Greece*. 4 vols. Translated by W. H. S. Jones. LCL. 1918–1935.

Philo. 14 vols. Translated by F. H. Colson and G. Whittaker et al. LCL. 1929–1953.

Philostratus. *Life of Apollonius of Tyana*. Translated by F. C. Conybeare. LCL, 1912.

_____. *Lives of the Sophists*. Translated by W. C. Wright. LCL, 1922.

Quaestiones in Genesim. Edited by F. Petit. Paris: Cerf, 1978.

_____. *Questions and Answers on Exodus*. Edited by J. B. Aucher, *Philonis Judaei paralipomena armena*. Venice: Coenobium PP. Armenorum, 1826. Tr.R. Marcus. LCL, 1953.

Plato. 12 vols. Translated by H. N. Fowler et al. LCL. 1914–1935.

Pliny. *Letters and Panegyricus*, vol. 2. Translated by B. Radice. LCL. 1969.

Pliny. *Natural Hisory*. 10 vols. Translated by H. Rackham et al. LCL, 1938–1962.

Plutarch. *Lives*. 11 vols. Translated by B. Perrin. LCL. 1914–1926.

_____. *Moralia*. 17 vols. Translated by F. C. Babbitt et al. LCL. 1927–1976.

Polycarp. See Apostolic Fathers.

Porphyry. *Porphyrius Philosophus Platonicus Opuscula Selecta*. Edited by
A. Nauck. Leipzig: Teubner, 1886. Reprinted, Hildesheim: Olms,
1963.

_____. *On the Cave of the Nymphs*. French translation in A. Buffière,
Les mythes d'Homère (Paris: Belles Lettres, 1956), 597–616.

Robinson, J. M. *The Nag Hammadi Library in English*. San Francisco:
Harper & Row, 1977.

Sappho. In *Greek Lyric*, vol. 1. Edited by D. A. Campbell. LCL. 1982.

Seneca. *Opera*. 3 vols. Edited by F. Haase. Leipzig: Teubner,
1884–1887.

_____. *Epistulae Morales*. 3 vols. Translated by R. Gummere. LCL.
1917–1925.

Seneca Rhetor. *Sententiae Divisiones Colores*. Edited by A. Kiessling.
Leipzig: Teubner, 1872.

Soranus. Edited by J. Ilberg. CMG 4. Leipzig and Berlin, 1927.

Stobaeus. *Anthologium*, Book 4. Edited by O. Hense. Berlin: Weidmann, 1909.

Stoicorum Veterum Fragmenta. Edited by H. von Arnim. 3 vols.
Leipzig and Berlin: Teubner, 1905 (reprint); vol. 4 (index) by M.
Adler, 1924.

Strabo. *Geography*. 8 vols. Translated by H. L. Jones. LCL.
1917–1932.

Suidae Lexicon. Edited by A. Adler. 2 vols. Leipzig: Teubner, 1928,
1931.

Tertullian. Corpus Christianorum: Series Latina 1, 1–2.

_____. *Traité du baptême*. Edited by R. F. Refoulé and M. Drouzy.
SC 35. 1952.

Theon. *Progymnasmata*. Edited by L. Spengel (Rhetores Graeci, 2).
Leipzig: Teubner, 1854.

Theophanes Continuatus. Edited by I. Bekker. CSHB 33. Bonn:
Weber, 1838.

Theophilus. *Ad Autolycum*. Edited by M. Marcovitch. PTS 44. 1995.

_____. *To Autolycus*. Edited by R. M. Grant. OECT. 1970.

Ulpian. *Die Epitome Ulpiani des Codex Vaticanus Reginae 1128*. Edited
by F. Schultz. Bonn: Marcus & Weber, 1926.

MODERN LITERATURE

Ameling, W. *Herodes Atticus*. 2 vols. Hildesheim: Olms, 1983.

Betz, H. D. *Galatians*. Philadelphia: Fortress, 1979.

Billerbeck, Margarethe. *Der kyniker Demetrius*. Philosophia Antiqua
36. Leiden: Brill, 1979.

Bonhöffer, A. *Epiktet und das Neue Testament*. Religionsgeschichtliche Versuche und Vorarbeiten 10. 1911.

Bonner, C. "A Dionysiac Miracle at Corinth." A J A 33 (1929), 368–75.

Botte, B. La *Tradition Apostolique de saint Hippolyte*. Liturgiewissenschaftliche Quellen und Forschungen 39. Münster: Aschendorff, 1963.

Bousset, W. "Eine jüdische Gebetssammlung im siebenten Buch der apostolischen Konstitutionen." NAG, 1915, 435–89.

Bouvrie, Synnøve des. "Augustus' Leigislation on Morals: Which Morals and What Aims?" *Symbolae Osloenses* 59 (1984): 93–113.

Broneer, O. "The Isthmian Victory Crown." *AJA* 66 (1962): 259–63.

———. "Paul and the Pagan Cults at Isthmia." *HTR* 64 (1971): 169–87.

Bruneau, P. "Isis Pélagia à Délos." *BCH* 85 (1961): 435–46; 87 (1963): 301–8.

Brusin, G. *Gli scavi di Aquileia*. Udine: Edizione de "La Panarie," 1934.

Cadbury, H. J. "Erastus of Corinth." *JBL* 50 (1931): 42–58.

———. "The Macellum of Corinth." *JBL* 53 (1934): 134–41.

Cadiou, R. *Commentaires inédits des Psaumes*. Paris: Belles Lettres, 1936.

Cauwelaert, F. R. van. "L'intervention de l'église de Rome à Corinthe vers l'an 96." *Revue d'histoire ecclésiastique* 31 (1935): 267–306.

Chadwick, H. "'All Things to All Men' (1 Cor.IX.22)." *New Testament Studies* 1 (1954–1955): 261–75.

Charlesworth, M. P. *Trade-Routes and Commerce in the Roman Empire*. Cambridge: Cambridge University Press, 1924.

Colson, F. H. "Notes on Justin Martyr, Apology I." *JTS* 23 (1921–1922): 161–71.

Conybeare, F. C. "The Kiss of Peace." *Expositor* 4, no. 9 (1894): 460–62.

Conzelmann, H. *Die Apostelgeschichte*. Tübingen: Mohr (Siebeck), 1963.

———. "Korinth und die Mädchen der Aphrodite." NAG. 1967.

Cook, R. M. "Ancient Greek Trade: Three Conjectures. 1. The Diolkos." *JHS* 99 (1979): 152–53.

Corbett, P. E. *The Roman Law of Marriage*. Oxford: Clarendon, 1930.

Dibelius, M. "Die Mahl-Gebete der Didache." *ZNW* 37 (1938): 32–41.

Dinsmoor, W. D. "The Largest Temple in the Peleponnesos." Hesperia Supplement 8 (1949): 104–15, with plate 15.

Dix, G. *The Shape of the Liturgy*. Westminster: Dacre, 1945.

_____. *The Treatise on the Apostolic Tradition of St Hippolytus of Rome.* London: SPCK, 1937.

Droge, A. J. and J. D. Tabor. *A Noble Death.* San Francisco: Harper-SanFrancisco, 1992.

Engels, D. *Roman Corinth.* Chicago: University of Chicago Press, 1990.

Feger, R. "Cicero und die Zerstörung Korinths." *Hermes* 80 (1952): 436–56.

Fiensy, P. *Prayers Alleged to Be Jewish: An Examination of the Constitutiones Apostolicae.* Brown Judaic Studies 65. Decatur, Ga.: Scholars Press, 1985.

Fimmen. "Isthmos." RE 9 (reprinted 1997): 2256–65.

Frank, T., ed. *An Economic Survey of Ancient Rome.* 5 vols. Baltimore: Johns Hopkins, 1938. Reprinted, Paterson, N.J.: Pageant Books, 1959.

Fridrichsen, A. "Peristasenkatalog und res gestae," *Symbolae Osloenses* 8 (1929), 78–82.

_____. "Zum Stil der paulinischen Peristasiskatalogs," *Symbolae Osloenses* 7 (1928), 25–29.

_____. "Zum Stil der Peristasenkatalogs," Kungliga Humanistika Vetenskaps-Samfundet i Uppsala, årsbok 1943, 287–89.

Gebhard, E. R. and M. W. Dickey. "The View from the Isthmus," in Corinth XX (forthcoming).

Gelinsky, K. "Augustus' Legislation on Morals and Marriage," *Philologus* 125 (1981), 126–44.

Gerster, B. "L'Isthme de Corinthe. Tentatives d'empercement dans l'antiquité." *BCH* 8 (1884): 225–32 (with plate 8).

Goodenough, E. R. *By Light Light: The Mystic Gospel of Hellenistic Judaism.* New Haven, Conn.: Yale University Press, 1935.

Graindor, P. *Un milliardaire antique: Herodes Atticus et sa famille.* Cairo: Misr, 1930.

Grant, F. C. *Hellenistic Religions.* New York: Liberal Arts, 1953.

Grant, R. M. *Early Christians and Animals.* New York: Routledge & Kegan Paul, 1999.

_____. *Gods and the One God.* Philadelphia: Westminster, 1986.

_____. "Neither Male nor Female." *Biblical Research* 37 (1992): 5–14.

_____. "Pliny and the Christians." *HTR* 41 (1948): 73–74.

_____. "The Structure of Eucharistic Prayers." *Antiquity and Humanity: Essays on Ancient Religion and Philosophy Presented to Hans Dieter Betz on His 70th Birthday,* eds. A. Y. Collins and M. M. Mitchell (Tübingen: Mohr, 2001), 321–32.

Grant, R. M. and H. H. Graham. *First and Second Clement.* New York: Thomas Nelson, 1964.

Gregory, T. E. *The Corinthia in the Roman Period.* Journal of Roman Archaeology Supplement 8. 1994.

Hammond, M. "Octavia (Minor)." RE 17:1859–68.

Hammond, N. G. L. "Roads. I. Greek." *Oxford Classical Dictionary,* 2d ed. Oxford: Clarendon, 1970.

Hanson, R. P. C. "The Liberty of the Bishop to Improvise Prayer in the Eucharist." *VC* 15 (1961): 173–76. Reprinted in *Studies in Christian Antiquity,* pp. 113–16. Edinburgh: T. & T. Clark, 1985.

Harris, W. V. "Child-Exposure in the Roman Empire." *Journal of Roman Studies* 84 (1994): 1–22.

Herter, H. "Die Soziologie der antiker Prostitution im Lichte des heidnischen und christlichen Schrifttums." *JAC* 3 (1960): 70–111.

Highet, G. *Juvenal the Satirist.* New York: Oxford University Press, 1961.

Hofmann, K. -M. *Philema hagion.* Gütersloh: Bertelsmann, 1938.

Horrell, D. G. *The Social Ethos of the Corinthian Correspondence.* Edinburgh: T. & T. Clark, 1996.

Humbert, M. *Le remariage à Rome.* Milan: Giuffrè, 1972.

Imhoof-Blumer, F., and P. Gardner. "Numismatic Commentary on Pausanias: Megarica, Corinthiaca." *JHS* 6 (1885): 59–77.

Jalland, T. G. "Justin Martyr and the President of the Eucharist." *TU* 80 (1962): 83–85.

Johnson, S. E. "Paul in the Wicked City of Corinth." *Lexington Theological Quarterly* 17 (1982): 59–67.

Kern, O. *Orphicorum Fragmenta.* Berlin: Weidmann, 1922.

Kroll, W. "Lesbische Liebe." RE 12 (reprinted, 1994): 2100–102.

Kunkel, "Matrimonium." RE 14 (1930): 2259–86.

Laporte, J. *La doctrine eucharistique de Philon d'Alexandrie.* Théologie historique 16. Paris: Beauchesne, 1972.

Leipoldt, J. "Agapen." Die Religion in Geschichte und Gegenwart 1, 3d ed., 1957.

Lenschau, "Korinthos." RE Supplement 4 (reprinted, 1992): 991–1036.

Lietzmann, H. *An die Korinther* I–II, 4th ed. Edited by W. G. Kümmel. Tübingen: Mohr (Siebeck), 1949.

———. "Ein liturgischer Papyrus des Berliner Museum." Festgabe für Adolf Jülicher (Tübingen: Mohr [Siebeck], 1927), 213–28.

———. *Messe und Herrenmahl.* Berlin: De Gruyter, 1926. (E. T. *Mass and Lord's Supper.* Translated by D. H. G. Reeve. Leiden: Brill, 1979).

Lutz, C. *Musonius Rufus the Roman Socrates.* Yale Classical Studies 4. 1947.

MacDonald, B. R. "The Diolkos." *JHS* 106 (1986): 191–95.

Malherbe, A. J. "Hellenistic Moralists and the New Testament." *Aufstieg und Niedergang der rîmischen Welt* 2.26.1. (Berlin: De Gruyter, 1992), 267–333.

_____. *Paul and the Popular Philosophers*. Minneapolis: Fortress, 1989.

Martin, D. B. *The Corinthian Body*. New Haven, Conn.: Yale University Press, 1995.

Mason, H. J. "Lucius at Corinth." *Phoenix* 25 (1971): 160–65.

Mazza, E. *The Origins of the Eucharistic Prayer*. Collegeville, Minn.: Liturgical Press, 1995.

Meyer, E. "Korinthos," KP 3 (1969), 301–5.

Mitchell, Margaret. *The Heavenly Trumpet: John Chrysostom and the Art of Pauline Interpretation*. Tübingen: Mohr (Siebeck), 2000.

Moxnes, H. *Constructing Early Christian Families: Family as Social Reality and Metaphor*. New York: Routledge & Kegan Paul, 1997.

Murphy-O'Connor, J. *St. Paul's Corinth: Texts and Archaeology*. Wilmington, Del.: Michael Glazier, 1983.

Nash, E. *Pictorial Dictionary of Ancient Rome*, 2d ed. 2 vols. New York and Washington: Praeger, 1968.

Nautin, P. "Apostolic Constitutions." *Encyclopedia of the Early Church*. Edited by A. DiBerardino. New York: Oxford University Press, 1992.

_____. *Lettres et écrivains chrétiens des iie et iiie siècles*. Paris: Cerf, 1961.

Newton, D. *Deity and Diet: The Dilemma of Sacrificial Food at Corinth*. Journal for the Study of the New Testament Supplement 169. 1998.

Nock, A. D. *Essays on Religion and the Ancient World*. Edited by Z. Stewart. 2 vols. Oxford: Clarendon, 1972.

_____. "Liturgical Notes." *JTS* 30 (1929): 381–95.

_____. "Pagan Baptisms in Tertullian." *JTS* 28 (1927): 289–90.

Oppermann, S. "Hafenanlagen." KP 2 (1967): 912–16.

Osiek, C. *The Shepherd of Hermas*. Minneapolis: Fortress, 1999.

Peek, W. *Der Isishymnus von Andros und verwandte Texte*. Berlin: Weidmann, 1930.

Pernot, L. *La rhétorique de l'éloge dans le monde gréco-romain*. 2 vols. Paris: Institut d'Études Augustiniennes, 1993.

Price, C. P. "Jewish Morning Prayers and Early Christian Anaphoras." *Anglican Theological Review* 43 (1961): 153–68.

Raepsaet, G. "Le Diolkos de l'Isthme à Corinthe: son trace, son fonctionnement." *BCH* 117 (1993): 233–56.

Robertson, N. "A Corinthian Inscription Recording Honors at Elis for Corinthian Judges." *Hesperia* 45 (1976): 253–66.

Romano, D. G. "Post-146 B.C. Land Use in Corinth, and Planning of the Roman Colony of 44 B.C." In *The Corinthia in the Roman Period*, edited by T. E. Gregory. Journal of Roman Archaeology Supplement 8 (1994), 9–30.

Roux, G. *Pausanias en Corinthie*, (*Livre II, 1 à 15*). Paris: Belles Lettres, 1958.

Saffrey, H. D. "Aphrodite à Corinthe: Réflexions sur une idée reçue." *Revue Biblique* 92 (1985): 359–74.

Saxer, V. *Rites de l'initiation chrétienne du iie au vie siècles*. Spoleto: Centro italiano di studi sull'alto medioevo, 1988.

Schermann, T. *Griechische Zauberpapyri und das Gemeinde- und Dankgebet im I.Klemensbriefe*. TU 34.2b, 1909.

Segelberg, E. "The Ordination Prayers in Hippolytus." Studia Patristica 13 (1975): 397–408.

Skutsch, F. "Ein neuer Zeuge der altchristlichen Liturgie." *Archiv für Religionswissenschaft* 13 (1910): 291–305.

Smith, D. E. "The Egyptian Cults at Corinth." *HTR* 70 (1977): 201–31.

Spawforth, A. J. S. "Roman Corinth: the Formation of a Colonial Elite." In *Roman Onomastics in the Greek East* (MELETEMATA 21), edited by A. D. Rizakis. Athens and Paris: Boccard, 1996.

Stillwell, R. "The Theatre at Corinth." *AJA* 33 (1929), 77–97.

Story, C. I. K. "Justin's Apology I. 62–64: Its Importance for the Author's Treatment of Christian Baptism." *VC* 16 (1962): 172–78.

Stroud, R. S. "The Sanctuary of Demeter and Kore on Acrocorinth. Preliminary Report I: 1961–1962." *Hesperia* 34 (1965): 1–24 and plates 1–11.

Talley, T. J. "From *Berakah* to *Eucharistia*: A Reopening Question." *Worship* 50 (1976): 115–37.

———. "The Eucharistic Prayer of the Ancient Church according to Recent Research: Results and Reflections." *Studia Liturgica* 11 (1976): 138–58.

———. "The Literary Structure of the Eucharistic Prayer." *Worship* 58 (1984): 404–20.

Taubenschlag, R. *The Law of Greco-Roman Egypt in the Light of the Papyri 332 B.C.–640 A.D.* New York: Herald Square, 1944.

Thraede, K. "Friedenskuss." *RAC* 8 (1972): 505–19.

———. "Ursprünge und Formen des 'Heiligen Küsses' im frühen Christentum." JAC 11/12 (1968/69): 124–80.

van den Hoek, A. "Aristobulus, Acts, Theophilus, Clement Making Use of Aratus' Phainomena: A Peregrination." *Bijdragen* 41 (1980): 290–99.

van der Waele. "Korinthos." RE Supplement 6 (reprinted 1997): 182–99, 1350–51.

van Geytenbeek, A. C. *Musonius Rufus and Greek Diatribe.* Assen: Van Gorcum, 1963.

Van Unnik, W. C. "Les cheveux défaits des femmes baptisées." *VC* 1 (1947): 77–100.

_____. "1 Clement 34 and the 'Sanctus.'" *VC* 5 (1951): 204–48.

_____. "Studies over de zogenaande eerste brief van Clemens 1. Het litteraire genre." Mededelingen der Koninklijke Nederlander Akademie van Wetenschappen, Nieuwe Reeks 33.4. 1970.

Verdelis, N. M. "Der Diolkos am Isthmus von Korinth." *Athenische Mitteilungen des Deutschen Archäologischen Instituts* 71 (1956): (33–41), 51–59.

_____. "Die Ausgrabungen des Diolkos wèhrend den Jahre 1957/59."*Athenische Mitteilungen des Deutschen Archäologischen Instituts* 73 (1958): (95–107), 140–45.

von Fritz, K. "Musonius." RE 16 (1933): 893–97.

Weiss, J. *Der erste Korintherbrief.* Gîttingen: Vandenhoeck & Ruprecht, 1910.

Wendland, P. *Quaestiones Musonianae.* Berlin: Mayer et Mueller, 1886.

Westermann, W. L. "Sklaverei." RE Supplement 6 (reprinted 1997): 894–1068.

Williams, C. K., II. "Roman Corinth as a Commercial Center." In *The Corinthia in the Roman Period,* edited by T. E. Gregory. Journal of Roman Archaeology Supplement 8 (1994), 31–46.

Winter, B. W. *Seek the Welfare of the City: Christians as Benefactors and Citizens.* Grand Rapids: Eerdmans, 1994.

Wiseman, J. "Korinth und Rom 1: 228 B.C.–A.D. 267." *Aufstieg und Niedergang der römischen Welt* 2.7.1. Berlin: De Gruyter, 1979.

_____. *The Land of the Ancient Corinthians.* Studies in Mediterranean Archaeology 50. Göteborg: Aström, 1978.

Youtie, H. C. "The *Kline* of Sarapis." *HTR* 41 (1948): 9–29.

Zeegers-Vander Vorst, N. *Les citations des poètes grecs chez les apologistes chrétiens du iie siècle.* Louvain: Publications Universitaires, 1972.

Index of Biblical References

Index of Ancient Writers and Writings

Index of Subjects